Acknowledgments

Sincere thanks go to my colleagues at Edith Cowan University, especially Sean Monahan and Ken Willis, for ideas and encouragement; to Bronwyn Mellor for her thoughtful reading of the chapters and for text suggestions; to Wayne Martino, Annette Patterson, John Richmond and Helen Savva for reading and commenting on the manuscript; to Stephen Mellor for design and layout; and to my wife Annette for constant support.

This book is dedicated to my parents,
Roy and Florence Moon,
with thanks.

About the author

Brian Moon taught English in Western Australian secondary schools before completing a PhD in the area of literary theory. He has served on English syllabus committees and has been an examiner of English for the Secondary Education Authority. He now lectures in English curriculum studies at Edith Cowan University in Perth, Western Australia.

He is author of *Studying Literature: Theory and Practice for Senior Students* and *Literary Terms: A Practical Glossary* also published by Chalkface Press.

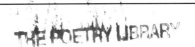

TO THE TEACHER

This book offers an approach to poetry study that is different from other textbooks currently available. The majority of poetry texts used in schools today fall into two categories: anthologies, which generally offer little in the way of practical guidance for poetry study, and 'experience-oriented' resource books, which often emphasise performance and personal response over analysis. Many of these books make excellent resources, but in both types an attachment to Romantic conceptions of poetry often narrows the ways in which students are encouraged to explore poetry texts.

This book openly emphasises analysis and inquiry, though without ignoring the connections poetry can have to individual and social experience. It treats poetry not as a mystical, heightened mode of expression but as a form of discourse. It argues that poetry, like all discourses, is governed by conventions of thought and action that are embedded in historical and social contexts. By making some of these conventions explicit, the book tries to give students a clearer understanding of how poetry works. Instead of leading students through a study of decontextualised terms and concepts, the book examines poetry in terms of the beliefs and values, practices and contexts that writers, readers, publishers and teachers work with and within.

The six chapters that follow have a roughly sequential structure that leads from experience, through exploration, to theorisation; but individual chapters and sections can be used equally well in isolation, to fit in with each teacher's preferred approaches and programs of study.

Chapter 1 introduces poetry study through shared readings of poems that students themselves choose. In part, this is an attempt to break down some of the antipathy that students may have built up toward poetry. But the chapter goes beyond the 'experience' approach, to show that readings and performances of poems are themselves forms of analysis, and that such activities also function as interventions in the construction of meaning from poems.

Chapter 2 invites students to investigate the 'nature' of poetry. This section of the book introduces the idea of poetry as discourse: that is, the idea that poetry is not merely a kind of writing with inherent qualities, but a set of *practices* (of reading, teaching, publishing, and so on) related to certain kinds of social action and interaction.

Chapters 3 and 4 lead students through practical activities in the reading and writing of poetry. Chapter 3 introduces the ideas of word and connotation, while Chapter 4 focuses on the relationship between forms, meanings and the social functions of poetry. These chapters take a 'workshop' approach to the reading and writing of poems offering students practical methods for analysing and constructing poetic texts.

Chapter 5 provides models and guidelines for writing *about* poetry. This section will be especially useful for students in senior years who have to write formal analyses and critiques of poetry texts. It offers annotated examples of student critiques, as well as step-by-step guidelines that students can follow in their own writing.

Finally, **Chapter 6** introduces students to some theoretical accounts of poetry. It shows how ideas about poetry are related to social and historical contexts, and how specific critical methods are developed to deal with specific forms of poetry. The chapter introduces students to the thinking of some influential theorists, from Plato to Roland Barthes. The aim in this section is not to turn students into 'theorists', but to show that there are different ways of looking at poetry, none of which is natural or timeless. This material will be most suitable for senior students, and teachers may find it helpful to work through a study of the various theories over a period of weeks, perhaps devoting part of one class each week to reading and discussion of a particular critical orientation.

STUDYING

POETRY

WITHDRAWN FROM THE POETRY LIBRARY

Brian Moon

Chalkface Press

First published in Australia in 1998

Chalkface Press Pty Ltd
PO Box 23
Cottesloe WA 6011
AUSTRALIA

The acknowledgments on pages 154 and 155 constitute
an extension of the copyright notice.

Every effort has been made to trace and acknowledge copyright.
The publishers apologise for any accidental infringement and
would welcome information to correct the situation.

The National Library of Australia
Cataloguing–in–Publication data:

Moon, Brian, 1958–
Studying Poetry

Includes index.
ISBN 1 875136 20 7

1. Poetics.   2. Poetry – Explication.   I. Title.

808.1

Edited by Bronwyn Mellor
Designed by Stephen Mellor

Cover: *Buch mit zwei Augen [Book with two eyes]* (1964) Hubertus Gojowczyk;
© 1964 The artist. All rights reserved.

Typeset by Chalkface Press

Published in Britain by The English & Media Centre, 18 Compton
Terrace, London N1 2UN

Printed in Britain by Redwood Books

CONTENTS

1.

Performing Poetry

PEAS

I eat my peas with honey,
I've done it all my life.
It makes the peas taste funny,
But it keeps them on the knife.

Anonymous

ABOUT THIS BOOK

This book aims to get you thinking about poetry in different ways. It tries to challenge some of the common ideas that people have about poetry. The main idea of the book is that poetry is not simply a special form of writing. In this book poetry is treated as an *activity* that people sometimes take part in, just as they sometimes read novels or go to movies or build houses or play sport.

In this book it is assumed that people can use poetry for different purposes on different occasions: to entertain; to make money; to think philosophically about life; to sell a product; to make a political point; to mark a special occasion. This view of poetry differs from the traditional idea that poems are always about personal feelings and experiences, and 'deep' meanings.

As you work through the following chapters you will learn to study poems in terms of their structures, patterns, and uses, as well as their 'literary' meanings. Along the way you will find yourself asking questions that might not have occurred to you before.

In the chapters to come you will get involved in the following activities, and more.

- Constructing 'readings' of poems by presenting them aloud.
- Surveying the poetry preferences of people in your class.
- Testing different definitions of poetry.
- Analysing the sounds, words and forms of poetry texts.
- Writing your own poems by working from models.
- Writing formal critiques (studies) of poems.
- Reading and applying different theories of poetry.

Getting started

A good way to begin studying any subject is to start with what you know – and what you like. So this book begins by asking you to think about the kind of poems you like, and to share them with others in your class. Sharing poems in this way, and talking about which ones you like or don't like, can raise interesting questions – about what you think poetry is, why people read and write poems, and how they make sense of them. Answering some of those questions is what this book is about.

Activity

Before you start work on this chapter, here are some questions to write about or discuss.

1. What do readers expect to find in poems?

2. Where are most people likely to encounter poems in their everyday lives? (Your answer may depend on how you define a 'poem'.)

3. What kind of poems do readers most enjoy?

Favourite poems

Most people can think of at least one poem that they have read or heard and enjoyed – even those who don't like poetry. Many people even know a poem by heart.

Your poem may be one you recall from childhood, or it may be associated with some important experience or person in your life. It could even be a poem you have studied in school. You might like the poem because it is amusing, or because it means something special to you, or because you like the sound of it.

If you can't think of a favourite poem, here are some ideas to choose from that may help.

Find a poem in this book (or a poetry anthology) that you think is interesting.

Choose one of the following to share with the class:

- a song lyric;
- a greeting card verse;
- a rhyme that helps you remember things (such as the months of the year).

Choose a poem that you *don't* like – and be prepared to say why.

Activity

1. Bring a copy of your poem to class, to share with your group.

2. Start your presentation by introducing the title of your poem and the writer's name.

3. Read your poem to the group, and explain why you like (or dislike) it. In your explanation you might comment on the following:

   - how and when you discovered the poem;
   - aspects of the poem that you like (the sound? the words? the images? something else?);
   - anything about the poem that you don't like.

A class poetry survey

The poems you have shared can tell you something about the kinds of poetry that people in your class enjoy.

Use a survey table similar to the one on page 10 to record the features of the poems that were shared in your class.

Activity

1. First, fill in the table for *your poem* only by placing a tick in the appropriate boxes. (Note: You may need to practise reading your poem aloud to be sure about some aspects of its sound.)

2. Transfer your results to a *class copy* of the table. (This could be drawn on the board or on a large sheet of paper that can be pinned up for everyone to see). Tally the class results in the second column.

   The survey results should allow you to draw some general conclusions about what you and your classmates look for in a poem. For example, how many of the people in your class prefer poems that rhyme? How many chose 'serious' poems?

POETRY SURVEY		
Features	**Your poem**	**Your class's poems**
REGULAR RHYME Tick if the lines rhyme in some kind of pattern.		
STRONG RHYTHM Tick if the poem has a 'beat' that is more rhythmical than everyday speech.		
FREE VERSE Tick if the poem has no rhyme, and no obvious rhythm.		
LONG Tick if the poem is 20 lines or more in length.		
SHORT Tick if the poem is less than 20 lines long.		
NARRATIVE Tick if the poem tells a story of some kind.		
DESCRIPTIVE Tick if the poem concentrates on description rather than storytelling.		
HUMOROUS Tick if the poem is amusing and fun to read.		
SERIOUS Tick if the poem deals with its subject in a serious way.		
EMOTIVE Tick if the poem uses words that encourage an emotional reaction.		
'LITERARY' LANGUAGE Tick if the poem uses unusual, complex or 'flowery' language.		
PLAIN LANGUAGE Tick if the poem uses plain, everyday language.		
PLEASANT SOUNDING Tick if the poem's sound is a strong part of its appeal.		
VISUALLY INTERESTING Tick if the poem's layout on the page is part of its appeal.		

You may photocopy this page. Studying Poetry

POETRY READINGS

A useful way to begin studying poems is through prepared readings or performances. In preparing to read a poem aloud for an audience you need to think carefully about its sound and meaning, and this is a good first step in the study of any poem.

Through performance you also are constructing a specific interpretation or *reading* of the poem that others can react to, and this is a good way to generate discussion.

Practice readings

Reading aloud for an audience is something that most people find a little frightening at first. The short exercises in this section will give you some practice. To make the experience enjoyable for your listeners you may need to use more volume and variation in your voice than normal.

Below are some short humorous poems called *limericks*. This form of verse takes its name from a county in Ireland, which featured in an old song 'Oh Will You Come Up to Limerick'. Limericks are often dismissed as 'light' verse, but they have very strict rules for structure and content, and they can be very demanding to write.

The following activity asks you to use these limericks to practise reading aloud.

Activities

1. Working in small groups or pairs, take turns reading *one* of the following short poems to your partner/s. Concentrate on making your voice clear and loud, and try not to speak too quickly. Alternatively, you may wish to use a tape recorder to hear your own performance.

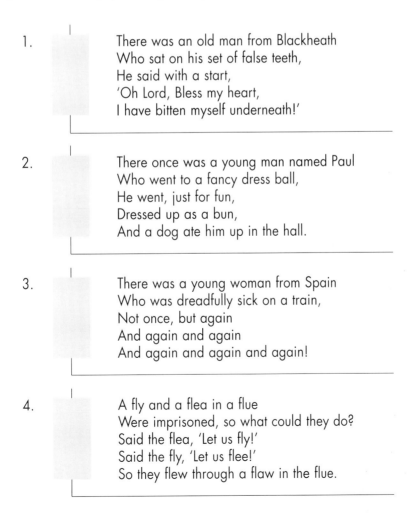

1.   There was an old man from Blackheath
     Who sat on his set of false teeth,
     He said with a start,
     'Oh Lord, Bless my heart,
     I have bitten myself underneath!'

2.   There once was a young man named Paul
     Who went to a fancy dress ball,
     He went, just for fun,
     Dressed up as a bun,
     And a dog ate him up in the hall.

3.   There was a young woman from Spain
     Who was dreadfully sick on a train,
     Not once, but again
     And again and again
     And again and again and again!

4.   A fly and a flea in a flue
     Were imprisoned, so what could they do?
     Said the flea, 'Let us fly!'
     Said the fly, 'Let us flee!'
     So they flew through a flaw in the flue.

2. Now choose one of the poems to read in chorus with your partner/s. You will need to concentrate on:

        – keeping in time together;

        – matching your volume and expression.

Before you start reading, note where the *stresses* or rhythmical beats are in each line, and discuss which words or phrases should be emphasised in your reading. The stresses have been underlined for you in the following example.

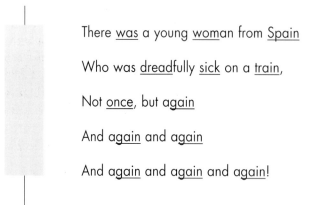

There <u>was</u> a young <u>wo</u>man from <u>Spain</u>

Who was <u>dread</u>fully <u>sick</u> on a <u>train</u>,

Not <u>once</u>, but a<u>gain</u>

And a<u>gain</u> and a<u>gain</u>

And a<u>gain</u> and a<u>gain</u> and a<u>gain</u>!

This pattern of stresses is the same for all of the previous limericks.

3. Practise reading your chosen poem with different amounts of emphasis, until you are satisfied that your reading is clear. Once again, you might find a tape recorder useful to check on your performance.

4. You should also try varying the volume and expression of your voice. Practise reading the 'woman from Spain' text in each of the following ways:

        – with emphasis on the word 'dreadfully';

        – in an increasingly despairing tone;

        – in an increasingly astonished tone;

        – in an increasingly weakened tone.

5. Try similar variations in reading the other texts. What effects do these variations have?

Thinking about sound

Sound, which includes features such as pitch, speed, rhyme and rhythm, can be important in shaping the way we read a poem, and the meanings we make from it.

Activity

The short texts on the next page are different kinds of poem. They have been written, largely without punctuation, in paragraph form to disguise their appearance.

The activity asks you to reconstruct the texts as poems. This is in order to help you consider the importance of sound in your reading of poetry. As well as asking you to decide where the lines of the texts might begin and end when written as poems, the activity also encourages you to think about how your reading of a text may be affected by its layout on the page. (You can compare your decisions with the originals on page 151.)

1. Rewrite the texts below as poems, making your own decisions about where the lines will begin and end. You will find it helpful to read the text aloud as you work.

1. A man who weighed many an ounce used language I dare not pronounce for a fellow unkind pulled his chair from behind just to see so he said if he'd bounce.

   (Anonymous)

2. On the planet of Nim in the quadrant of Zax lives a blue-bearded Bodge that the locals call Max he lives all alone in a ramshackle duff and he spends his days lunching on yaffetter fluff now a Bodge is a very strange creature indeed for his body is covered in Evergreen weed (it's a little like mould and a little like moss and a little like lichen – except for the gloss) but a bearded Bodge well he's one of a kind and his Evergreen coat although shortish behind sweeps down from his chin like a river of gold (except that it's *blue* as I'm sure you've been told).

   ('The Bearded Bodge,' Dr Brain)

3. The sea is calm tonight the tide is full the moon lies fair upon the straits – on the French coast the light gleams and is gone the cliffs of England stand glimmering and vast out in the tranquil bay come to the window sweet is the night-air only from the long line of spray where the sea meets the moon-blanch'd land listen! you hear the grating roar of pebbles which the waves draw back and fling at their return up the high strand begin and cease and then again begin with tremulous cadence slow and bring the eternal note of sadness in.

   (From 'Dover Beach,' Matthew Arnold)

2. When you have finished, compare your reconstructed poems with others in your group or class, then discuss these points.

   a. How important was sound in helping you reconstruct the layout of the text?

   b. What types of sound did you make use of? (rhymes? pitch? others?)

   c. What other clues, if any, did you rely on?

   d. How does the layout of the text – as paragraph or verse – influence your reading of it?

Guided presentations

This section contains two poems for presentation, along with guidelines that will help you through your first poetry performance.

There also are activities to help you think about your readings of the poems and, therefore, about your *interpretations* of them.

Read the first poem 'Gutter Press', by Paul Dehn on the next page. We can read this poem as a comment on the kind of stories that are reported in newspapers and television broadcasts.

The news editor speaks in the kind of headlines we often associate with sensational stories; the cameraman has a different style of speaking.

GUTTER PRESS

News editor:

        Peer Confesses,
Bishop Undresses,
Torso Wrapped in Rug,
Girl Guide Throttled,
Baronet Bottled,
JP Goes to Jug,

        But yesterday's story's
        Old and hoary,
        Never mind who got hurt.
        No use grieving,
        Let's get weaving,
        What's the latest dirt?

Diplomat Spotted,
Scout Garrotted,
Thigh Discovered in Bog,
Wrecks Off Barmouth,
Sex in Yarmouth,
Woman In Love With Dog,
Eminent Hostess Shoots Her Guests
Harrogate Lovebird Builds Two Nests.

Cameraman:

        Builds two nests?
Shall I get a picture of the lovebird singing?
Shall I get a picture of her pretty little eggs?
Shall I get a picture of her babies?

News Editor:

                              No!
Go and get a picture of her legs.

Beast Slays Beauty,
Priest Flays Cutie,
Cupboard Shows Tell-Tale Stain,
Mate Drugs Purser,
Dean Hugs Bursar,
Mayor Binds Wife With Chain,
Elderly Monkey Marries For Money,
Jilted Junkie Says "I Want My Honey".

Cameraman:

        "Want my honey?"
Shall I get a picture of the pollen flying?
Shall I get a picture of the golden dust?
Shall I get a picture of a queen bee?

News Editor:

                              No!
Go and get a picture of her bust.

Judge Gets Frisky,
Nun Drinks Whisky,
Baby Found Burnt in Cot,
Show Girl Beaten,
Duke Leaves Eton –

Cameraman:

        Newspaper Man Gets Shot!
May all things clean
And fresh and green
Have mercy upon your soul,
Consider yourself paid
By the hole my bullet made –

News Editor:

(dying) Come and get a picture of the hole.

Paul Dehn

1. 'Gutter Press' could be performed by two people taking the parts already indicated in the text. Or it could be prepared as a group reading. Work in pairs or small groups to prepare a reading of 'Gutter Press', using the guidelines below.

For two readers

Choose one person to read the news editor's lines and one to read the cameraman's. Practise reading the poem aloud using different voice styles for each speaker. Experiment with volume and expression to help convey the poem to your audience. You will need to build up to the shooting by portraying the cameraman's increasing exasperation.

For a small group

For a group reading, the 'headlines' spoken by the editor can be read by different group members, with one person reading the cameraman's lines and another reading the editor's instructions to the cameraman. In this way the poem can be divided up as follows:

Lines	1–6	Group members take turns to read one line each.
Lines	7–12	Editor only, speaking to himself.
Lines	13–20	Group members take turns.
Lines	21–24	Cameraman only.
Lines	25–26	Editor only, speaking to the Cameraman ... and so on.

2. Present your reading to the class, and compare the different approaches that have been used by different readers.

What do the readings show?

In preparing your performances of 'Gutter Press' you have had to study the poems carefully. You will have made decisions about what the poem might mean and what purposes it might be used for (eg, to entertain people, to raise questions about the role of the media, and so on).

Activity

1. Discuss the questions below about the way the poem was presented by readers in your class.

   a. What kind of voices did readers use for the editor and cameraman?

   Was the editor's voice:

aggressive?	☐	loud?	☐
soft?	☐	fast?	☐
slow?	☐	accented?	☐
male?	☐	female?	☐
exaggerated?	☐	stereotyped?	☐
innocent?	☐	other?	☐

   Was the cameraman's voice:

aggressive?	☐	loud?	☐
soft?	☐	fast?	☐
male?	☐	female?	☐
slow?	☐	accented?	☐
exaggerated?	☐	stereotyped?	☐
innocent?	☐	other?	☐

   b. Discuss the reasons for using these voices, referring to the poem to explain your decisions.

2. Which of the following statements best describes the way the cameraman and the news editor are portrayed, according to your reading of the poem?

   a. The editor is ruthless and only cares about selling papers; the cameraman is more sensitive and cares about people.
   b. The editor is realistic and knows what readers want; the cameraman is sentimental and very naive about the world.
   c. The editor is doing his job; the cameraman is being deliberately unhelpful.
   d. The editor is being serious; the cameraman is mocking him.
   e. The news editor regrets the kind of stories he must report; the cameraman enjoys them.
   f. The editor and cameraman both enjoy their work; they are playing around and mocking critics of the media.

   Support your decision with 'evidence' from the text that backs up your reading.

3. Based on your reading, which of the following ideas does the poem seem to support?

   a. The media prefer to report scandal, not real news.
   b. The media are run by corrupt individuals.
   c. Newspaper readers prefer scandal over real news.
   d. Newspaper readers are corrupt individuals.
   e. Modern society has no real values and is degenerating into sleaziness.
   f. Modern society has a healthy enjoyment of sex and scandal.

Re-reading the text

In most classes there will be strong agreement about what this poem means and how it should be read. Many readers will assume that their reading is 'obvious' and is supported by the text itself. But is it really so clear? The following activities encourage you to reconsider your initial reading.

Activities

1. Choose an alternative reading (one that disagrees with your initial reading) of the poem, from the list in question 2 at the top of this page. Working in pairs or groups, discuss how the poem could be presented so as to support this new reading.

2. Ask volunteers to present their alternative reading to the class, then consider these questions.

   a. How easy or difficult is it to read the poem in a new way?

   b. What aspects of the text help or hinder this reading?
      (Specific words? Punctuation marks? Layout?)

3. If the poem could be read in a range of alternative ways, why do most readers initially read the poem in a *similar* way? The following are some possible reasons. Discuss these in your groups. Suggest other reasons if you can.

   a. The meaning is clear from the words on the page. Alternative readings only come from 'twisting' the words.
   b. Readers already have a stock of ideas about the media and news editors, and they use these to make sense of the poem.
   c. Readers always expect poems to support traditional values (such as attacking the media) so they automatically read the poem in a way that matches these values.
   d. Schoolteachers often use literature to encourage students to take a critical view of the media, so readers in a classroom automatically use the poem in this way.

Misunderstanding and Muzak

This poem can be read as the thoughts of two people who have got their meeting plans confused.

MISUNDERSTANDING AND MUZAK

You are in the Supa Valu supermarket
expecting to meet me at 6.15.

I am in the Extra Valu supermarket
expecting to meet you at 6.15.

Danny Boy is calling you down special-offer aisles.
Johann Strauss is waltzing me down special-offer aisles.

I weigh mushrooms and broccoli and beans.
You weigh beans and mushrooms and broccoli.

It is 6.45. No sign of you.
It is 6.45. No sign of me.

You may have had a puncture.
I may have been held up at work.

It is 6.55. You may have been murdered.
It is 6.55. I may have been flattened by a truck.

Danny Boy starts crooning all over you again.
Johann Strauss starts dancing all over me again.

Everything that's needed for our Sunday lunch
is heaped up in my trolley, your trolley.

We hope to meet somewhere, to eat it.

Dennis O'Driscoll

Reading the poem

You can apply what you have learned from your work on 'Gutter Press' on page 14 to prepare a reading of this new poem.

Activities

1. Read through 'Misunderstanding and Muzak' with a partner and decide which lines or phrases should be spoken by each character. (This might not be as obvious as it seems.) The final line could be read by both of you together.

2. Rehearse your reading a number of times, trying a range of different approaches. For example, you could experiment with each of the following emotions and expressions.

       amusement   anger   hostility
       frustration   panic   contempt

   You may think of different ideas that the poem could be used to support.

3. Present the readings to the class, and discuss the ideas and views that each group's readings seem to support.

Your own presentation

For your own presentation you could use one of the 'favourite' poems you have shared in your class, or one of the poems you have worked with in this chapter. You may also wish to browse through a range of poetry collections to find a new poem that you like.

You could give presenters useful feedback on their performance by filling in a table similar to the one below.

AUDIENCE RESPONSE SHEET	
PRESENTER(S)	
TITLE OF POEM	
VOICES Were the presenters' voices: – loud and clear enough? – expressive enough?	
PRESENTATION Did the presenters: – introduce the poem clearly? Were the presenters: – confident? – enthusiastic? – well organised?	
INTERPRETATION Did the approach taken work for this poem? Why/why not?	
SUMMARY What was the best feature of the presentation? What advice would you give for improving the presentation?	

RADICAL READINGS?

You have seen how reading poems in different ways can achieve different effects. Poetry performers can take advantage of this fact to make a specific argument or statement through their presentation of a poem.

In this section you will see how a poem can be used to support *or* to challenge specific cultural beliefs and values.

You may photocopy this page.

The Soldier

'The Soldier,' by English poet Rupert Brooke, was written in 1914, while Brooke was serving with the British Navy in World War I. Traditionally it has been read as a very stirring and patriotic piece of writing.

THE SOLDIER

If I should die, think only this of me:
That there's some corner of a foreign field
That is for ever England. There shall be
In that rich earth a richer dust concealed;
A dust whom England bore, shaped, made aware,
Gave, once, her flowers to love, her ways to roam,
A body of England's, breathing English air,
Washed by the rivers, blest by suns of home.

And think, this heart, all evil shed away,
A pulse in the eternal mind, no less
Gives somewhere back the thoughts by England given;
Her sights and sounds; dreams happy as her day;
And laughter, learnt of friends; and gentleness,
In hearts at peace, under an English heaven.

Rupert Brooke

Exploring the poem

The activities that follow will help you to think about ways of reading 'The Soldier'.

Activities

1. Printed below is a jumbled paraphrase of the poem, in which short sections of the poem have been re-written in simpler language. Working with a partner, number the sections from 1 to 6, to show their correct order. The first section has been numbered for you.

	Things seen and heard, friendship and peace, and pleasant thoughts that make England what she is.
1	If I die, this is what I want you to think about me: that my grave is a little bit of England in a foreign land.
	As I turn to dust, my body will enrich that foreign soil with a touch of England.
	My body became part of England, absorbing the sun, air and waters of England.
	England gave birth to me, educated me, gave me the pleasure of her natural beauty, and the freedom to wander and grow.
	And as I decay, in peace at last, I bring to this foreign land those elements of England that I am composed of:

2. Now you have read the poem carefully, practise reading it aloud in a serious, patriotic style. Experiment with volume, tone, accent, speed, and intonation to create the right effect.

Our youth in arms

Sir Winston Churchill was an admirer of Brooke. He once said that no other poet had captured so well 'the nobility of our youth in arms'. His words support a patriotic reading of 'The Soldier' by suggesting that the death of men in wartime is a noble sacrifice. This view is part of a set of beliefs about war, death, youth and national pride often promoted in times of conflict.

Activities

1. Which of the following beliefs do you think are supported by Churchill's words and by patriotic readings of Brooke's poem? Make a note of your selections.

    a. The young are the most important members of a society.
    b. Young men are the most important members of a society.
    c. A death in war is a good death.
    d. A death in war is a bad death.
    e. Dying in a war is the kind of death most men want.
    f. Dying in a war is the kind of death most men *should* want.
    g. War is a glorious event.
    h. War is an inescapable fact of life.
    i. War is a waste of human life.
    j. England is the most civilised country on earth.
    k. The British Empire achieved greatness through aggression and colonisation.

2. Discuss these beliefs with others in your class and create an agreed list. What is your reaction to these views?

An alternative view

For those who disagree with these views about war, death and youth, a patriotic reading of 'The Soldier' might be distasteful or even offensive. These people might want to offer a different reading of the poem – one which does not produce the traditional patriotic view of war.

Activities

1. How could you reject or 'unsettle' the patriotic reading of Brooke's poem by changing your presentation of it? Here are some possible approaches for re-reading 'The Soldier'.

    a. Reading in an increasingly crazed, raving voice that suggests the soldier has lost touch with reality.
    b. Exaggerating the patriotic reading to the point where the speaker sounds foolish, misguided or just silly.
    c. Reading in a bitter voice that suggests the speaker is mocking the ideas and beliefs represented in the poem.
    d. Reading as a specific character – such as a British football hooligan.

    Discuss these ways of reading the poem, and see if you can suggest other possibilities.

2. Practise different approaches to reading the poem, and discuss the different effects of each.

3. Return to some of the poems you have read in this chapter, and reconsider your original approach to the reading. Start by identifying some of the beliefs that the reading seems to support, then consider ways of changing the presentation to challenge those beliefs.

Discussion

Are there right and wrong ways of reading a poem? If so, how would we know which way is right? If not, how would you choose between readings?

2.

What is Poetry?

CURSE OF THE PEAR-SHAPED FIGURE

The Lord's no Michaelangelo,
I'm slim at the top but I'm fat below.

MIDDLE-AGED SPREAD

God sure wasn't no Givenchy,
My legs are slim but my waist is paunchy.

THE GOOD LORD

The Good Lord wasn't no Versace,
My neck is fine but my collar is starchy.

Deborah Andrews
(For Alan Jackson)

WHAT IS POETRY?

In your work so far you have been sharing poems with others in your class. To do this you have had to assume that everyone *knows* what a poem is. In the work that follows you are asked to think more carefully about poems, and about what poetry is.

Write a definition

Is there something about poetry that makes it different from other kinds of writing?

Before reading on, try writing your own definition of poetry.

_____

_____

Share your ideas with others in your group or class. Try to arrive at an agreed definition.

When you have finished, write down your group or class definition.

_____

_____

Activity

Testing your definition

On pages 23 and 24 there are six texts for you to read. They have been printed without titles, authors or descriptions.

1. Working on your own, read all of the texts and decide which of them, *according to your definition,* are poems. Record your decisions in a table like the one below. (Fill in only the columns for 'Your decision' and 'Your reasons' at this stage.)

Text	Is it a poem? (Y/N)		Reasons	
	Your decision	Group decision	Your reasons	Group reasons
1.				
2.				
3.				
4.				
5.				
6.				

2. When you have finished, compare your choices with others in your group or class. If there are disagreements, discuss the reasons for your choices and try to come to an agreed decision for each poem. Record these 'majority' decisions in the 'Group decision' column of the table, along with the reasons for the choices.

1.

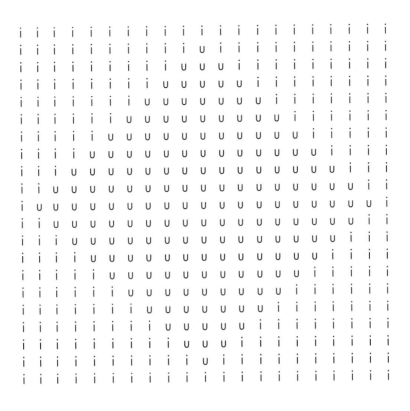

2.
Death will be so quiet and peaceful
Death reminds me of reincarnation
Death reminds me of sleep
Every day I step into a coffin

3.
That man over there say a woman needs
to be helped into carriages and lifted over ditches
and to have the best place everywhere.

Nobody ever helped me into carriages
or over mud puddles …
And ain't *I* a woman?
Look at me. Look at my arm.
I have ploughed and planted
and gathered into barns
and no man could head me …
And ain't I a woman?
I could work as much and eat as much as a man –
when I could get to it – and bear the lash as well,
And ain't I a woman?
I have borne thirteen children
and seen most all sold into slavery
and when I cried out a mother's grief
none but Jesus heard me
And ain't I a woman?

4.

```
                          r-p-o-p-h-e-s-s-a-g-r
                  who
        a)s w(e loo)k
        upnowgath
                  PPEGORHRASS
                              eringint(o-
        aThe):l
              eA
                !p:
        S                                        a
                      (r
        rIvInG                    .gRrEaPsPhOs)
                                          to
        rea(be)rran(com)gi(e)ngly
        ,grasshopper;
```

5.

```
        abcd
        efg
        hijk
        lmnop
        qrs
        tuv
        wx
        y & z
```

6.

Try to remember the kind of September
When life was slow and, oh, so mellow.
Try to remember the kind of September
When grass was green and grain was yellow.
Try to remember the kind of September
When you were a tender and callow fellow.
Try to remember and if you remember,
Then follow, follow, follow.

Some of the pieces you have just read are poems taken from poetry books. Others are different forms of writing or snippets of text taken from elsewhere. This list gives you the details of each piece.

1. Poem: 'The Affair', by Alan Riddell.
2. Lines from the alphabetical index of a poetry book.
3. Speech rendered as a poem: 'Ain't I a Woman' (extract) by Sojourner Truth.
4. Poem: 'r-p-o-p-h-e-s-s-a-g-r', by E. E. Cummings.
5. The letters of the alphabet.
6. Pop song: 'Try to Remember' (extract), by Tom Jones and Harvey Schmidt.

Discussion

How accurate were you in sorting the poems from the non-poems? Did your definition *always* help you make the right choice? If not, can you alter the definition to make it more accurate?

Other definitions

When people ask the question 'What is poetry?' they usually mean, 'What are the textual *features* that make a piece of writing a poem?' In practice it isn't so easy to say what these features are. Many poems have regular rhyme, or a definite rhythm; but others seem to have no regular features at all. They may look like jumbled collections of words or letters.

Here are some other definitions of poetry. Read through them, keeping *your* definition of poetry in mind. Then do the activities that follow.

> Poetry is the best words in the best order.
> *Samuel Taylor Coleridge*

> Poetry is the art of rhythmical composition, written or spoken, for exciting pleasure by beautiful, imaginative or elevated thoughts. *Macquarie Dictionary*

> Poetry is a form of writing in which few lines run right to the edge of the page.
> *Unknown*

> Poetry is generally esteemed the highest form of literature.
> *A.E. Housman*

> Poetry is the spontaneous overflow of powerful feelings … recollected in tranquillity.
> *William Wordsworth*

> Poetry is what gets lost in translation.
> *Robert Frost*

> Poetry is the record of the best and happiest moments of the happiest and best minds.
> *Percy Bysshe Shelley*

> A form of writing in which the writer is concerned with the organisation of lines as well as the meaning of words. *Encyclopedia Britannica*

1. Definitions of poetry often fall into two categories. Some are descriptions of features (such as sound, or rhyme). Others seem to be statements of value or belief. Try sorting the definitions on the previous page into these two categories. One example is given.

Value-definitions	Feature-definitions
Percy Bysshe Shelley	

2. Test some of these definitions against the texts on pages 23 and 24.

   a. How useful are they in sorting poems from non-poems?
   b. Say which definition is most useful, and which is least useful.
   c. Do you find one approach more convincing than the other – values or features?

3. Go back to your class or group definition. Does it refer to features, values or a combination of both? Is there anything about it that you now want to change?

POETIC READING

Because the differences between individual poems are so great, it is very difficult to define poetry solely in terms of *features* such as the presence of rhyme or the use of imagery. There always seem to be poems that break the rules of any definition.

Perhaps it is not only the features of some texts that make them 'poetry', but also our *reading* of them. We could say that 'poems' are pieces of writing that are offered to us for reading in poetic ways.

Of course, this raises another problem – how to define 'reading in a poetic way'.

Activity

1. Think about *how* you read poetry. What things do you think, do, feel when reading poetry that you *don't* do when reading other kinds of text? The following list might help get you started. When reading poetry, do you:

   – expect it to be boring?
   – read aloud rather than silently?
   – expect it to be difficult?
   – look for a 'deep' meaning?
   – feel emotions?
   – expect it to rhyme?

   Write down the items on the list that apply to you, then see how many points you can add.

2. Compare your list with a partner, or with others in your class or group.

Poetry reading rules

Following is a list of some things that readers are commonly taught to do when reading poetry. Compare this list with the one you made about how *you* read poetry. Can you add to this list?

	Poetry reading rules
1.	Pay attention to the language; for example, sounds, repetitions, patterns.
2.	Pay attention to the layout of the text.
3.	Recognise certain conventions or features; for example, metaphor, symbol.
4.	Look for ambiguous, surprising or contradictory meanings.
5.	Look for a general comment about life, or society, or people.
6.	Reflect on individual experiences, values or feelings about the subject.
7.	
8.	

Reading in a poetic way

If 'poetry' is at least partly an effect of how we read, it should be possible for us to read *other* texts – those not usually thought of as poetry – in poetic ways.

Below is an everyday text that was not written as a poem, but which we could try to read in poetic ways. It is a shopping list.

> veges – POTATOES
> something for lunch
> bananas
> bread
> coffee
> chicken fillets??
> go to the bank!

Here, for example, are some ways of reading the shopping list in a poetic way. We could:

- imagine a particular tone of voice for the message (bored? despairing?);
- use changes in the typeface as a guide for emphasis (focussing on the capitals in line one);
- search for ambiguous meanings by looking for words that can be read in different ways;
- look for patterns of similar sound, or feelings that you get from the sound;
- look for meaningful links between items on the list (perhaps the last line can be read as a comment on the cost of chicken fillets);
- look at the ideas in the poem as if they refer to 'life in general,' not just shopping (we could read the 'poem' as a comment on the triviality of our daily activities – or as a comment on poverty).

Activity

1. With these ideas in mind, practise reading the shopping list aloud, as if it were a poem. Experiment with changes of expression, volume, pace and so on, to bring out different meanings from this 'poem'.

2. Share your reading with others in your class or group, and discuss the effects of different 'performances'.

Guiding the reader

If poetry is partly a way of reading texts, we can say that poems are texts which have been designed to support a *poetic reading practice*. In this usage a 'practice' is a skill, or a routine way of doing something. This way of thinking about how we read poetry (as a routine way of doing something) can also help us to write poems.

Unlike most novels and stories, poems often use techniques of spacing, line-length, typescript and layout to generate meaning. These techniques can be used to help guide the reader's 'performance' of the poem, just as musical notation tries to guide a musician's performance.

For example, here is a telephone company invoice. Below it is the invoice re-written using the same words, but with changes to the layout and typeface.

Read through each text, then consider the questions that follow.

CHARGES AND PAYMENT

You must pay the charge shown on the account, which We will forward to You within 30 days of the due date. The final charge, as shown on the account, may be more or less than the total shown on this Service Statement because of adjustments reflecting discounts or concessions.

Please ensure that You pay the amount shown. If You do not pay by the due date, We may take action against you to recover the cost of our service.

CHARGES AND PAYMENT

you must pay the charge
shown on the account
which We will forward to you
within 30 days
of the due date

the   **Final Charge**,
(as shown on the account)
may be more
or less
than the total shown on this
   Statement
because of adjustments reflecting
discounts or concessions.

Please ensure that you pay the
   Amount Shown

If You do not pay by the
   Due Date
We may take
action against you –
to recover the cost of our

   Service

Kim Poulton

Activity

1. Read the invoice aloud. Then read the 'poem', 'Charges and Payment' aloud. How does your reading of it differ from your reading of the invoice?

2. Practise reading the 'poem' aloud. How do the line divisions, spacings and changes in typeface such as capitalisation of some words affect your reading?

3. How do these factors influence the meaning you make from the text? Do the changes encourage you to make meanings that weren't there before? If so, what meaning does the text now seem to have?

The writer comments

The following commentary was written by Kim Poulton, the student who produced the 'poem' based on the 'Charges and Payment' text. Read through her comments and see how successful she has been in shaping your reading of the text.

At first I wasn't sure what to do with this, so I started by just dividing the lines up in different ways until they were easy to read, without any jumps in the meaning between lines. Then as I thought about the words, I felt that the telephone company was trying to bully its customers, even though they always pretend to be such friendly people. So I thought about emphasising all the legal sounding words that usually are printed on telephone bills. I did this by using bold type. Then I got the idea of lining up all the bold type words in a column, like they might appear on a bill.

The final word is 'service', but I wanted to show that this column of bullying words doesn't add up to service! So I moved that word across the page more, so that it stood out on its own. I wanted to make the reader pause, so that they would think about the real meaning of service, and how it doesn't fit with the rest of the message. I want people who read the poem to see that there is a difference between service and bullying.

In order to construct her 'poem', Kim Poulton has read the original text in a poetic way. We can see evidence in her commentary, and in the changes she has made to the original text.

Activity

1. What were the 'poetry reading rules' Kim Poulton followed in her reading? Look back through her poem and commentary, and see which of the following rules have been used. If you find evidence that a rule has been used, note this in the right-hand column.

	Poetry reading rules	Evidence
1.	Pay attention to the language (eg, sounds, repetitions, patterns).	
2.	Pay attention to the layout of the text.	
3.	Recognise certain conventions or features (eg, metaphor, symbol).	
4.	Look for ambiguous, surprising or contradictory meanings.	
5.	Look for a general comment about life, society, or people.	
6.	Reflect on individual experiences, values or feelings about the subject.	

2. Discuss how well Kim Poulton achieved her aims with this 'poem'. Has she produced a text that you can read in a poetic way?

   If you think she did not succeed, what reasons can you give for this? Can you suggest ways of changing her poem so that it would be more successful?

Finding a poem

'Finding' poems hidden in ordinary pieces of writing or speech can be interesting and fun. It can also raise important questions about the way rules, situations and expectations influence our reading of a text.

Printed below is a piece of legal text, taken from a membership contract for a health club. Read through the text using poetic reading techniques, such as keeping an eye out for interesting sounds, words, patterns and ideas.

> I hereby declare that my membership details are true and correct. I shall not be entitled to refunds for any reason. This membership is not transferable. I hereby warrant that I am physically and medically fit. I agree to abide by the rules. If at any time I am guilty of misconduct, I may have my rights and privileges cancelled without notice. I acknowledge this agreement cannot be cancelled before the end of the minimum period of twelve months. I hereby declare that I have read and understood the conditions.

Activity

1. Try creating your own poem by re-shaping the way this text is laid out on the page. You could try using the following techniques:
   - dividing the text into shorter lines;
   - using boldface, italic or capitals for some words;
   - changing the spacing of words and lines;
   - changing the punctuation;
   - creating a pattern in the text;
   - inventing a title for the text.

   With these techniques you can guide the way a reader 'performs' the text.

   You will find it helpful to try reading the text aloud in variety of different ways. Try altering such things as your:
   - speed;
   - rhythm;
   - expression;
   - emphasis.

   See how these changes affect the meaning of the text.

2. When you have finished, write a paragraph of explanation, like the one written by Kim Poulton on the previous page. Say what your poem means to you, and explain how you tried to bring out this meaning.

3. Swap poems with someone else in your class or group. Practise reading each other's poems, and discuss how successful you have been in guiding your reader's performance.

Borrowed language

Some poets write poems by imitating or mocking certain kinds of language, such as legal documents and rule books.

The following poem, by British poet Raymond Wilson, imitates some aspects of the language of an official letter. Read the poem, then work through the questions that follow.

THIS LETTER'S TO SAY

Dear Sir or Madam
This letter's to say
Your property
Stands bang in the way
Of Progress, and
Will be knocked down
On March the third
At half past one.

There is no appeal,
Since the National Need
Depends on more
And still more Speed,
And this, in turn,
Dear Sir or Madam,
Depends on half England
Being tar-macadam.
(But your house will –
We are pleased to say –
Be the fastest lane
Of the Motorway).

Meanwhile the Borough
Corporation
Offer you new
Accommodation
Three miles away
On the thirteenth floor
(Flat Number Q
6824).

But please take note,
The Council regret:
No dog, cat, bird
Or other pet;
No noise permitted,
No singing in the bath
(For permits to drink
Or smoke or laugh
Apply on Form
Z 327);
No children admitted
Aged under eleven;
No hawkers, tramps
Or roof-top lunchers;
No opening doors
To Bible punchers.

Failure to pay
Your rent, when due,
Will lead to our
Evicting you.
The Council demand
That you consent
To the terms above
When you pay your rent.

Meanwhile we hope
You will feel free
To consult us
Should there prove to be
The slightest case
Of difficulty.

With kind regards,
Yours faithfully ...

Raymond Wilson

Activity

Discuss or write short answers to these questions.

a. In what ways does the poem imitate or mock the language of an official letter?

b. How does the poem guide your reading 'performance'? What features of the language and layout are involved?

c. What does this poem seem to be saying? What meanings came through in your reading of it?

d. How did the poem attempt to guide your reading? What role was played by:

  – the poem's imitation of an official letter;
  – the actual content of the 'letter';
  – the layout;
  – patterns of sound and word meaning;
  – other features?

POETRY-EFFECTS?

In this chapter you have seen that it is difficult to define poetry as simply a specific form of language or writing, or as a specific kind of text, because there is so much variation between the language and structure of individual texts called poems. There seem to be very few features that are shared by all poems. It can be helpful, therefore, to think about poetry as being, in part, a way of reading – one that involves responding to words, sounds, typeface and other features in particular ways and in adopting particular 'approaches' to the text, such as using the poem to reflect on your experiences and beliefs.

This suggests that poetry is not simply a form or kind of text, but something more complex: a combination of textual features, reading practices, beliefs and values. Different combinations of these can lead to quite different poetry 'experiences'. We could speak about different 'poetry-effects' resulting from different combinations of text, language, and ways of reading.

Activating practices

If poetry is at least partly a matter of how we read, and not only what is written on the page, how do we know when to switch *on* our poetry reading practice, and when to switch it *off*? And how do we know what kind of reading to do – personal, analytical, emotional or practical?

Activity

Below is a list of factors that *might* be involved in activating your poetic reading practice. Working in groups, decide which of these factors might encourage you to 'read in a poetic way'. (Note: you might not always be aware of these factors at the time.)

Use this code to indicate the degree of influence each item might have.

1 = very important   2 = moderately important   3 = unimportant

	Factors	Importance		
		1	2	3
1.	How the text is laid out on the page.			
2.	The kind of book that the text is contained in.			
3.	A teacher's announcement that the text is a poem.			
4.	Recognising the writer's name.			
5.	Your purpose in reading the text.			
6.	The subject matter of the text.			
7.	Aspects of the language in the text.			
8.	Your physical location (schoolroom, home etc).			
9.	The writer's purpose in writing the text.			
10.	Your educational training.			
11.	The title of the text.			
12.				
13.				
14.				

Can you think of other factors that might be important in telling you to read the text as a poem? If so, add these to the list, and indicate their importance.

A poetry chart

The chart at the bottom of the page shows how one combination of elements can result in a particular 'poetry-effect'. Above it are lists of elements that could be combined to produce other 'poetry-effects'.

Activity

1. On your own, choose some different types of poem and use the lists to fill in other possible 'poetry-effects' on a chart. You may find that many combinations are possible even for a single kind of poem, or a single way of reading. You may wish to add other types of poems and features to the lists. You could include poems you have studied in class.

Textual features	Reading practices	Poetry-effect produced
Regular rhymes No rhyme Strong rhythms Weak rhythms Typeface variations Large print Illustrations Fixed line/stanza lengths Narrative (story) Description Metaphor, simile etc Interesting sounds Unusual word order Oral text Printed text	Reading aloud (eg, to a child) Reading silently Reading at bed-time Reading in school Reading for pleasure Reading for information Reading for sound Reading for meaning Reading for philosophical reflection Reading for fantasy/escapism Reading for a single meaning Reading for multiple meanings Reading for a personal message Reading for personal reasons Reading as a set task	Emotion Boredom Self-indulgence Resistance Anxiety Practical action Learning Amusement Self-reflection Reflection on life Annoyance Confusion Enjoyment Admiration Sadness

Type of poem	Common examples	Textual features	Reading practices	Poetry-effect produced
Nursery rhymes	'Jack & Jill' 'Eensy Weensy Spider'	Strong rhymes Playful use of sound Story-based Accompanying illustrations and actions	Read aloud Read for fun Focus on sound Not analysed Read to/with children	Enjoyment Love of word-sounds Knowledge of rhymes
Ballads				
Limericks				
Greeting cards				
War poems				
Obituaries				
Love poems				
Sonnets				

2. When you have filled in your chart, compare your entries with those of others in your group or class. Do others have combinations that you didn't consider?

Context and use

Arguments that suggest poetry is a way of reading often become circular. It might seem that our poetic reading practice is triggered by a certain factor, such as rhythm. But for this to happen, we must already know to 'read for rhythm', otherwise we wouldn't register it. So it seems we must have already decided to read in a poetic way ...

Reading contexts

One way around this problem is to recognise that texts never ambush us when we are completely unprepared. All of our reading activities take place within specific *contexts* that guide us in our reading, even *before* we see the text on the page.

For example, your reading of the poems in this book has been governed by a great many factors that shape how you will approach the texts. Some of these are listed below.

> The classroom situation.
> The instructions of your teacher.
> The school timetable.
> The English curriculum.
> The title of this book.
> The instructions and activities that surround each poem.
> The layout and presentation of the texts.

These factors form a network of procedures, purposes, expectations and values that guide your reading of the texts. They tell you to switch on your poetry reading practice before you even look at the text.

Using texts

A reading context doesn't only tell readers what kind of text they are reading. It can also set up a particular *use* for the text.

For example, if you consult an instruction manual to find out how to work a new camera, it is unlikely that you will respond emotionally to the beauty of the words. Instead of using the text to stir your emotions, you will use it to find out which button takes the picture or focuses the lens.

This doesn't mean that the manual cannot be read for pleasure or emotion. We can imagine a context in which someone might read it in this way. For example:

> an old person looking back at the manual, remembering her first camera, and enjoying the recollection of reading the manual;

> or

> archaeologists of the future, stumbling across the camera manual and using it to gain a glimpse of a lost civilisation and its writings.

These examples are somewhat extreme, but there are similar situations that demonstrate this point just as clearly.

To His Coy Mistress

The following poem, 'To His Coy Mistress', was written in 1681 by Andrew Marvell, an English poet. It generally is read as a passionate lover's plea for his mistress to give in to his desires.

Read the poem through once, then do the activities that follow.

TO HIS COY MISTRESS

Had we but world enough and time,
This coyness, lady, were no crime.　　　　　　(coyness = coldness)
We would sit down and think which way
To walk, and pass our long love's day.
Thou by the Indian Ganges' side
Should'st rubies find; I by the tide
Of Humber would complain. I would
Love you ten years before the flood,
And you should, if you please, refuse
Till the conversion of the Jews.
My vegetable love should grow
Vaster than Empires and more slow;
An hundred years should go to praise
Thine eyes, and on thy forehead gaze;
Two hundred to adore each breast,
But thirty thousand to the rest;
An age at least to every part,
And the last age should show your heart.
For, lady, you deserve this state,　　　　　　(state = stateliness, dignity)
Nor would I love at lower rate.
　　But at my back I always hear
Time's winged chariot hurrying near;
And yonder all before us lie
Deserts of vast eternity.
Thy beauty shall no more be found;
Nor, in thy marble vault shall sound
My echoing song; then worms shall try
That long-preserved virginity,
And your quaint honour turn to dust,
And into ashes all my lust:
The grave's a fine and private place,
But none, I think, do there embrace.
　　　Now therefore, while the youthful hue
Sits on thy skin like morning dew,
And while thy willing soul transpires　　　　　(transpires = exhales)
At every pore with instant fires,
Now let us sport us while we may
And now, like amorous birds of prey
Rather at once our time devour
Than languish in his slow-chapped power.　　　(chapped = jawed)
Let us roll all our strength, and all
Our sweetness up into one ball,
And tear our pleasures with rough strife
Through the iron gates of life:
Thus, though we cannot make our sun
Stand still, yet we will make him run.

Andrew Marvell

To help you with your reading of 'To His Coy Mistress', the first twenty lines have been paraphrased for you below.

1. Working with a partner, place these paraphrased lines of the poem in order by numbering them from 1 to 7. The first has been numbered for you.

      ☐   I would tell you I had loved you since time began;
              and you could refuse me until all Jews became Christians.

       1   If we had all the time in the world, your
              playing 'hard to get' wouldn't be a problem.

       ☐   I would devote a whole century to looking at your
              beautiful eyes, two hundred years to each breast,
              and thousands of centuries for the rest of you, until
              finally I had captured your heart.

       ☐   We could sit around, go for walks, decide how we
              wanted to pass the time.

       ☐   My love for you would flower and grow with time like
              a vast empire.

       ☐   You could collect precious stones in far-off places,
              and I could mope by the river.

       ☐   You deserve such a dignified courtship, and I wouldn't
              want to rush things.

2. Read the poem again, from start to finish. Discuss the second half in your groups, and briefly summarise the speaker's argument.

Exploring uses

There are many ways of *using* a text like 'To His Coy Mistress'. Consider these uses of the poem.

1. A reader uses the text to study the conventions of love-poetry in the seventeenth century, comparing it with other similar poems.

2. A reader writes out the poem by hand, on expensive paper, and mails it to a boyfriend or girlfriend on Valentine's day.

These different *uses* of the text also imply different ways of reading it. One reader treats the poem as a historical document; the other as a persuasive argument. Thus, reading it, the readers above might do any of the following. (Which might each reader do when reading the poem?)

    – compare the lover's feelings to their own;
    – look for examples of romantic imagery;
    – identify common seventeenth century word usages;
    – focus on the romantic 'message' of the poem;
    – search for similarities to poems by Marvell's contemporaries.

Activity

The activity that follows asks you to think about other ways of using this poem, and how these uses might influence how the poem is read.

1. Choose *four* of the following uses, and say what aspects of the text you would focus on, and how you would read it.

   a. If you were studying how the English language has changed through history, and how word meanings have shifted:

      – what would you focus on?
      – how might you read?

   b. If you were in a romantic relationship, and wanted to reflect on your feelings:

      – what would you focus on?
      – how might you read?

   c. If you were studying the way people lived in 17th century Britain, especially their ideas about love and relationships:

      – what would you focus on?
      – how might you read?

   d. If you wanted to explore issues of sexism in the teaching of literature:

      – what would you focus on?
      – how might you read?

   e. If you wanted to explore Marvell's skill as a poet:

      – what would you focus on?
      – how might you read?

   f. If you were doing a psychological study of Marvell:

      – what would you focus on?
      – how might you read?

   g. If you were reading to enjoy the cleverness of the language and ideas:

      – what would you focus on?
      – how might you read?

   Discuss your answers with others in your class.

2. These different ways of reading the poem would be associated with different reading contexts. The reader who sends this poem to a girlfriend or boyfriend is acting within a context that we might call 'romantic courtship'. Try to describe the context of the four uses you have examined above. Some possible contexts are historical research; language study; cultural studies; biographical research; personal pleasure.

Summing up

It seems that in different reading contexts, the poem can become a different kind of 'object,' depending on how it is *used*. In the case of the Valentines, the poem seems to serve as a personal message or gift. In other contexts a poem could become a time machine, a personal journal, a historical document, or a cultural artefact. It could be used, for example, to recapture past feelings about a relationship, or as a trigger for a reader's thoughts and emotions, or as a source of information about the English language, or as a 'window' on life in the 17th century.

It seems that how we read poems (and other texts) is shaped by the contexts we are acting within, and by other social practices that we engage in – such as historical research, personal reflection, romance, and so on. Reading practices are ways of producing certain things – knowledge, states of mind and feeling, and arguments.

From this we can see that poetry is not simply a category of texts, but a complex set of activities that people engage in.

Poetry projects

These projects ask you to apply the work you have done in this chapter, and in Chapter One.

1. Found poems

Create your own 'found' poems. Find some texts with interesting uses of language and create poems by re-shaping the material.

You could try working with one or more of the following.

A copy of the school rules.   A sign in a public place.
A book index.   A newspaper article.

2. Borrowed language

Write a poem that imitates or mocks a specific kind of language.

Start by collecting and reading examples of texts with interesting forms of language. For example, you could use instruction manuals or legal documents and letters or television news broadcasts. Take note of the way language is used in your chosen text. Your poem may be more interesting if it makes a point about some issue that readers can reflect upon.

The following examples might serve as useful starting points:

   1.   A *recipe* or *set of instructions* giving instructions for a successful life.

> Collect the ingredients:
> one dash of learning,
> a hint of ambition ...

   2.   A *legal document* setting out a rules for relationships.

> The parties to this contract
> Are pleased to make it known
> That mutual attraction ...

   3.   A *TV news broadcast* reporting on the discovery of life beyond television.

> And now in news that's just come in:
> A fascinating story,
> That life exists beyond the tube ...

3. An anthology

Compile a group or class-illustrated anthology of poems, with commentaries from the writers.

Organise a poetry reading of works written in your class. Individuals or groups could present performances of their own or each other's poems.

4. Writing a definition

Your work in this chapter may have challenged your ideas about what poetry is, and how easy or difficult it is to define poetry. Try writing a new definition of poetry in the light of this work.

3.

Words
and
Meanings

RECKLESS

Last night I was reckless –

didn't brush my teeth

and went to bed tasting my dinner all night.

And it tasted good.

Pete Brown

BASIC INGREDIENTS

It can be argued that the basic ingredients of poetry are words and ways of reading them – though other elements such as layout, spacing and punctuation are also important. In this chapter you will explore some of the ways that readers and writers interact with words to produce the kinds of meanings and effects that are recognised as poetry.

The words used in a poem perform a complex task. They are chosen by writers to describe or 're-present' objects and ideas that the writer wishes to communicate about; and they are used by readers to construct meanings on the basis of certain reading practices. In some ways, words function as the common 'currency' that writers and readers use to create and exchange meanings. But, in other ways, it seems that writers and readers each work independently with the words to produce their own versions of the text.

This chapter contains projects and activities that will help you to explore the function of words in a poem from the reader's perspective. In the first section you will explore the way word meanings are shaped by different contexts and ways of reading. In later sections you will study how readers interact with words in specific poems.

Whose meanings?

The use of particular words in a poem will influence a reader's responses, and the meanings he or she produces, depending upon how the reader processes the text. Different words can result in different shades of meaning or feeling. For this reason, poets choose their words carefully, predicting how readers will react to certain choices and combinations.

The task of finding the 'right word' is made more difficult by the fact that different readers may respond in different ways to the *same* combination of words. This can be shown by inviting different readers to record the associations they make for particular words.

Below is one student's response to the word 'mother'. The student has written down all of the ideas and words that came into her mind when she thought of 'mother'.

Activity

1. Make your own idea-maps for the following words. Work quickly, and write down the first ideas that come to mind. Allow yourself 60 seconds for each map.

| father | home | police | school | sport |

2. Compare your responses with those of others in your class or group.

Private or public?

These idea-maps often contain a mixture of 'private' and 'public' responses. Some responses may draw on the reader's personal background (eg, a mother who wears glasses). Other responses seem to relate to a general idea of 'motherhood' that many people would recognise (eg, mother as a caring figure).

Activity

1. Go back to the 'mother' word map on the previous page and decide which responses are specific or private to this reader, and which seem more general or public.

2. Look at your own word-maps and decide which of your responses are private, and which public. You may find it useful to do this in groups, so that similarities can easily be spotted.

Different readers

These activities show how readers produce associations for words, and how readers can respond in different ways. These differences can affect not only personal responses, but also 'public' ones.

Here, for example, are summaries of two different responses to the word 'police'.

Police 1	Police 2
uniforms	hassles
car	badge
protection	gun
law	trouble
safety	worry

These differences could reflect different experiences. But they might indicate that the writers come from different places or social backgrounds (for example: country, inner city, suburbs) where the role of the police may be viewed differently by the community.

Different readings

The associations a reader has for a word can also change according to the situation, or context, in which it is used. For example, the same reader might produce different associations for the word 'mother' when working in a biology class and in a Food and Nutrition class.

Here are some possible associations that might arise in these contexts.

Mother 1	Mother 2
(Biology class)	(Food & Nutrition class)
female parent	kitchen
X chromosome	cooking
birth	shopping
reproduction	sewing
female hormones	caring

'Context', in this sense, refers to a form of *social activity* that involves certain kinds of behaviour, knowledge and language use. These contexts are sometimes called discourses – ways of speaking and acting within a culture or society.

1. Listed below is a set of associations for the word 'cat'. Match the associations with the three contexts by numbering each word with a 1, 2, or 3.
   (Some words may fit more than one context.)

Word:	Cat						
Contexts:	1. veterinary science 2. family life 3. nature conservation						
Associations:	feline		comfort		pest	
	friendship		work		lazy	
	killer		domestic pet		hungry	
	disease		invader		warmth	

2. Make up sets of associations for the following word and contexts.

Word:	Love					
Contexts:	1. religion 2. romance 3. science					
	1		2		3	
Associations:						

3. Compare your results with others in your group or class.

Life in general?

You have seen that the associations readers produce for a word can be influenced by:

- the reader's past experiences;
- the culture or society of the reader;
- the context in which the language is used.

These factors make it very difficult for writers of poetry to be sure that *all* of their readers will respond to a text by producing the 'right' meanings. Although writers may try to communicate ideas about 'life in general' it may be that there is no single view of life that all readers can share. This is one reason reading poetry can generate so much discussion and argument.

Some differences can be settled if readers agree to use 'standard' meanings of words – such as the meanings found in a dictionary, or the meanings thought to have been common at the time and place that the poem was written. But because poems continue to be read by a great variety of people, and long after they have been written, there will always be a degree of variation in the meanings that readers produce.

Readers need to become skilled at exploring the possible meanings that words and phrases can have, and at weighing up the possibilities. The activities that follow help you to look more closely at the meanings of words and phrases in a range of specific poems.

POEM COMPARISONS

One way of seeing how particular uses of language can shape a reading is by comparing different versions of the 'same' poem.

The following poem, 'First Frost', was written by the Russian poet Andrei Voznesensky. It has been translated into English by Stanley Kunitz.

The poem describes a girl whose feelings have been hurt by some event. She is alone in a telephone booth in wintery weather. The poem can be read as exploring themes about young love, relationships in general, or the hardships of growing up.

Read the poem, then do the activity that follows.

FIRST FROST

A girl is freezing in a telephone booth,
huddled in her flimsy coat,
her face stained by tears
and smeared with lipstick.

She breathes on her thin little fingers.
Fingers like ice. Glass beads in her ears.

She has to beat her way back alone
down the icy street.

First frost. A beginning of losses.
The first frost of telephone phrases.

It is the start of winter glittering on her cheek,
the first frost of having been hurt.

Andrei Voznesensky
(Trans. Stanley Kunitz)

Activity

1. Readers can produce a number of *themes* for this poem (a theme being a central meaning or message that the poem as a whole seems to explore). Which themes are most prominent in your reading of the poem? Select three themes from the following list, and list them in order from 1 (strong theme) to 3 (minor theme). You can add your own suggestions to the list if you disagree with these.

   Themes in 'First Frost'?

   a. the pain of young love;
   b. the failure of communication;
   c. the complexity of human relationships;
   d. women's experience of love;
   e. the trials of growing up;
   f. loneliness.

2. Compare your thematic reading with those of others in your class, giving reasons for your choices.

Frost or ice?

'First Ice' is another version of Andrei Voznesensky's poem, produced by a different translator, George Reavey. In his translation, Reavey has chosen slightly different words and phrases for his English version of the poem. These differences can affect the way readers respond to the text.

Read George Reavey's version of the poem, then do the activities that follow.

FIRST ICE

A girl freezes in a telephone booth.
In her draughty overcoat she hides
A face all smeared
in lipstick and tears.

She breathes on her thin palms.
Her fingers are icicles. She wears ear-rings.

She'll have to walk home alone,
Along the ice-bound street.

First ice. The very first time.
The first ice of telephone phrases.

Frozen tears glisten on her cheeks –
The first ice of human hurt.

Andrei Voznesensky
(Trans. George Reavey)

You will have noticed a number of differences between the two translations, including:

- different word choices (eg, 'flimsy' versus 'draughty');
- different phrasings/groupings of words (eg, 'stained by tears and smeared with lipstick' versus 'all smeared in lipstick and tears');
- the use of different tense forms of the present (eg, 'freezes' versus 'is freezing'), and so on.

Activities

1. Look for places where the words or phrases differ between the two texts, and decide quickly which wordings you think are better.

2. Make a list of your preferred wordings, thinking about your reasons for your choices.

3. Compare your choices with a partner, or with others in a small group. Give reasons for the choices you have made.

The activities that follow will help you think more carefully about your reactions to these two versions of the poem.

Sound and connotation

Readers of poetry can react to the choice of words in a poem in a number of ways. Two important elements that readers respond to are sound and connotation.

Sound

Some words may seem more appropriate than others because they have a *sound* which seems to match the general mood or subject matter of the poem. For example, words with 'round' vowel sounds or 'soft' consonants (like the word 'moon') often seem better for creating sad, quiet or reflective moods. Words with 'short' vowels or 'hard' consonants (like the word 'stock'), however, often seem better for creating happy, loud or active moods.

Activities

1. Sort these words into two lists: one for 'soft' sounds and one for 'hard' or harsh sounds. For this activity, try to ignore the meanings of the words. Compare your choices with others.

frost	pond	down	tick	flame	cut
bitter	lake	owl	rat	fire	fall
harm	deep	skittle	born	ice	mourn

2. Some techniques that use sound, which can be drawn upon by poets, are listed below on a chart. In column one is a list of terms; column two gives the meanings of the terms, and the third column gives examples. Some of the sections on the chart, however, have been left blank. Complete the chart by providing the missing term or meaning or example for each technique.

Term	Meaning	Example
	repetition of identical or similar consonants.	'Sliding, silently …'
assonance	repetition of similar or identical vowel sounds.	
	words that together make a discordant, harsh sound (usually sounds that are difficult to say together).	'La Jac Brite Pink Skin Bleach'
euphony	words that together make a pleasant, harmonious sound (usually sounds that are easy to say together).	
onomatopoeia		'The buzzings of the honey bees'

3. Discuss the effect of sound in the following two short 'mood poems'.

SLEEP

Dozing
Snoozing
Dreaming
Yawning
Sleeping

Stretching
Rolling
Curling
Folding
Sleeping

CITY SCENE

Heels tapping
Meters ticking
Brakes screeching
Buttons clicking
City life

Horns tooting
Lights flicking
Sirens hooting
I'm quitting
City life!

Connotation

Words can also affect the reading of a poem through the ideas and associations or *connotations* that readers produce for them. For example, the words, 'thin', 'lean', 'slightly built', and 'slender' all have a similar meaning, but they may suggest different associations to readers. For example, readers often react more positively to the word 'slender' than to the word 'thin'; and the former tends to be applied to women and boys, rather than to men.

Activities

1. Below are two combinations of words taken from the different versions of Andrei Voznesensky's poem. Tick the ideas and associations that each description suggests to you.

Words	Ideas and associations		Ideas and associations	
draughty overcoat:	full-length coat		old	
	half-length coat		worn out	
	loose fitting		thin	
	inexpensive		tattered and torn	
	lets in the cold air		coarse	
	borrowed/handed-down		other?	
flimsy coat:	full-length coat		old	
	half-length coat		worn out	
	loose fitting		thin	
	inexpensive		tattered and torn	
	lets in the cold air		coarse	
	borrowed/handed-down		other?	

Based on the ideas and associations you have ticked, which of the phrases ('draughty overcoat' or 'flimsy coat') do you think better matches the subject matter and mood of the poem, as you read it? Is sound also a factor in your choice?

2. Here are some other pairs of words or phrases from the two poems. Discuss the differences between them, taking account of sound and ideas. For each pair of phrases, say which you prefer (A or B).

	A	B	Your preference
1.	is freezing	freezes	
2.	huddles	hides	
3.	face stained by tears & smeared with lipstick	face all smeared in lipstick and tears	
4.	the start of winter glittering on her cheek	Frozen tears glisten on her cheeks	

3. In judging which of these words and phrases works better, you will have made some assumptions about the overall 'feeling' that readers should have about the girl and about her situation.

    Which of the following best describes this feeling, according to your reading of the poem?

Feeling	Explanation	Your reading
sympathetic	(the reader is *emotionally involved* and feels sorry for the girl)	
detached	(the reader merely *observes* the situation without feeling involved)	
understanding	(the reader *relates to* the situation but may not be emotionally affected)	
uninterested	(the reader *understands* the situation but has no particular view about it)	
philosophical	(the reader views the girl's situation in terms of *broader human experience*)	
other		

4. Does your idea about how the reader should feel help to explain the judgements you have made in the activities above?

    For example: would a preference for a *sympathetic* reading lead you to prefer particular words or phrases from the two different translations or versions of the poem over others?

    If so, where do you think your feelings about the character of the girl and her situation might have come from?

> The words in the poem?
>
> Personal experience?
>
> Stories and poems about similar situations?
>
> Movies?
>
> Somewhere else?

A reader's response

On the next page is a student's view of Andrei Voznesensky's poem. It is written in the form of a brief critical discussion, or critique. The writer is Greg Allan.

Read Greg Allan's critical discussion of both translations or versions of Andrei Voznesensky's poem carefully, then discuss the points that follow.

Reading "First Frost" and "First Ice"

Andrei Voznesensky's poem "First Frost" is about a young girl huddled in a telephone booth in the middle of winter. It seems that she has been heartbroken by news she has just received over the telephone, because the poem tells us she has experienced the "first frost of telephone phrases" (l. 10). She may have been betrayed or hurt by friends, or by a boyfriend, but we can't be sure because the poem doesn't give many details about this. The poem seems to be making a connection between the cold weather and the girl's feeling of being hurt. It says that being hurt by other people for the first time is like the beginning of winter in a person's life. This is put across in the last two lines, "It is the start of winter glittering on her cheek/the first frost of having been hurt" (l. 11–12). This makes me think that the **theme** of the poem is about the sadness of growing up and learning that other people can be cruel.

I think that each of the translators has been partly successful in getting this meaning across, but some lines in each poem work better than others. To begin with, the use of "is freezing" (l. 1) in "First Frost" is more effective than "freezes" because it seems to make the situation more alive for the reader, as if it is happening right now. The word "huddled" (l. 2) is also more effective than "hides" because it makes me think that the girl is doubled-up with her arms around herself, which would be true if she was cold and also if she was upset. But in lines three and four I think the second version of the poem, "First Ice" is better. "A face all smeared/in lipstick and tears" makes it sound as though the girl's tears and lipstick have all run together. In the other version, "stained by tears/and smeared with lipstick" keeps the two things separate, which goes against the idea of smudging. "A face all smeared in lipstick and tears" also reads more smoothly because of the similar sound of "smeared" and "tears".

The two versions of line six are also quite different. "Fingers like ice" is a good **comparison** because it seems to say that her fingers felt cold. The metaphor, "Her fingers are icicles" doesn't work as well because it seems to say that her fingers are not just cold but might also look like icicles, which can be sharp and harsh, and I don't think that is how the girl should be viewed. The use of "glass beads" for ear-rings is effective because the **image** of glass is a bit like ice, it is cold to the touch and you can see through it. Also, "beads" sounds more like the cheap jewellery that a very young girl would wear. "She wears ear-rings", on the other hand, is just a statement that doesn't seem relevant. It doesn't create any visual image or emotional feeling for the reader.

"First Frost" also has a much better conclusion than "First Ice". The reference to "winter ... on her cheek" helps the reader to make the connection between cold weather and feelings of hurt, so that the season of winter becomes a **symbol** for human hurt. But I think this could be improved by using the phrase "human hurt" from "First Ice" in the final line because it helps us read the poem as a more general comment on life, as if everyone has this kind of experience at some time.

Overall, however, I think that "First Frost" is the most effective version of the original poem, because it makes better use of sound and has more effective comparisons that help the reader to read the poem symbolically.

Greg Allan

Terms and concepts

In his discussion of 'First Frost' and 'First Ice', Greg Allan makes use of some concepts that are commonly applied when analysing poetry. They have been highlighted in his essay on page 48 in **bold** type. Below is a brief discussion of each concept.

Theme	This is a message or idea that the text as a whole seems to be concerned with, when read in a particular way. The theme is often an abstract idea (eg, love, sorrow) in contrast to the subject, which is more concrete (eg, girl in a phone booth).
Comparison	Comparison is where one object or idea is described in terms of its similarity to another object or idea. Common forms of comparison in poems include simile ('Fingers like ice') and metaphor ('It is the start of winter glittering on her cheek').
Image	An effective description, usually of an object; sometimes thought of as a mental picture. In this poem, 'glass beads' may be read as a good description of ear-rings, because it suggests a visual similarity to frozen droplets of water. Imagery, then, is used to make objects, feelings or ideas more concrete and powerful for the reader.
Symbol	The use of one object or idea to represent another. Sunshine often is used in poems to represent life, happiness, or youth. Winter is often used to symbolise death, sadness or age. Symbols are agreed on by certain members of a specific culture or group, so their meanings vary from time to time or place to place.

Activity

Do you agree with all of Greg Allan's comments on 'First Frost' and 'First Ice'?

1. Read through his essay with a partner, taking *one* paragraph at a time. For each paragraph discuss which ideas you agree or disagree with. You can record major points of agreement and disagreement by writing down the *line numbers* of relevant comments in the essay.

2. Record your findings in a table like this. An example has been done for you.

Paragraph	Agreements	Disagreements
1.	1. 6–8 cold weather & hurt	
2.		
3.		
4.		
5.		

Writing techniques

Greg Allan also uses a number of special techniques when quoting lines from the poems. These are *conventions* that critics and reviewers use, and which you should use in your own writing.

Activity

Listed below are four conventions used in Greg Allan's essay. Fill in the table by finding an example of each in his essay on page 48, then state the rule and explain its purpose. You should be able to work out the purpose of each rule from the essay.

Technique	Example	Purpose & rule
Quotation marks " "	lines 4, 9–10 ...	To show direct quoting from text. Wording must be accurately copied.
The slash /		
Details in brackets ( )		
The use of ellipsis . . .		

Essay structure

The structure and organisation of Greg Allan's essay could provide a model for your own writing.

The essay is developed in three main stages, as follows.

First paragraph (1)
An overview of the poem's subject matter, and the reader's view.

Middle paragraphs (2, 3, 4)
A detailed explanation of the reader's interpretation, supported by analysis of specific examples.

Final paragraph (5)
A brief summary of the main argument about the poem.

Refer back to Greg Allan's essay to see how the structure works in detail.

Paragraph structure

Each individual paragraph also has a clear structure. It begins with a *statement* about the poem, which is then *explained* and *supported* by examples.

Paragraph Four shows this structure very clearly:

Statement: "First Frost" … has a much better conclusion than "First Ice".

Explanation: The reference to "winter … on her cheek" helps the reader to make the connection between cold weather and feelings of hurt, so that the season of winter becomes a symbol for human hurt. I think this could be improved by using the phrase "human hurt" in the final line because it helps us read the poem as a more general comment on life, as if everyone has this kind of experience at some time.

Activity

There are some aspects of the poem that Greg Allan does not discuss in his essay, such as the difference between the phrases 'draughty overcoat' and 'flimsy coat' (l. 2).

Choose *one* aspect of the poem that you have an opinion on, and write one paragraph in which you state your opinion, explain and support the statement with examples. You can refer back to the activities above for ideas and evidence.

Statement:

Explanation:

Your version?

You may have found that there are parts of each translation of Andrei Voznesensky's poem that you like, and parts that you think are less effective.

Activities

1. Working alone or in pairs, create a new version of Voznesensky's poem by selecting your favourite lines, words and phrases from these two translations. Start by deciding which title you prefer: 'First Frost' or 'First Ice'. Then build up your version of the poem by combining the best parts of these two versions. (Remember to consider both sound and ideas in making your selections.)

    Write a neat copy of your 'adapted' poem.

2. Select volunteers from the class who are prepared to share their adapted poems. Have the volunteers write their poems on overhead projector sheets, or on the board, for easy display.

    Invite the volunteers to explain to the class *why* they chose specific words and phrases. Others in the class may wish to ask questions or comment on these 'new' poems.

A new 'translation'

Here is Greg Allan's adaptation of the translations by Stanley Kunitz and George Reavey of the poem by Andrei Voznesensky.

FIRST FROST

A girl is freezing in a telephone booth.
Huddled in her draughty coat she hides
A face all smeared
In lipstick and tears.

She breathes on her thin little palms,
Fingers like ice, glass beads in her ears.

She has to beat her way back alone
Along the ice-bound street.

First frost. A beginning of losses.
The first frost of telephone phrases.

It is the start of winter glittering on her cheek,
The first frost of human hurt.

Andrei Voznesensky
(Adapted by Greg Allan from the
translations of S. Kunitz and G. Reavey)

You might like to compare it with your own version and with those of other versions produced in your class.

CHANGING POEMS

Another way to explore the ways in which language in poetry 'works' is to make changes to existing poems. This can reveal a lot about the way a poem has been designed to invite a particular kind of reading or response.

In the first part of this section you will read a poem called 'Mushrooms', written by an American poet, Sylvia Plath.

Before going on to read the poem, however, you are asked to work through the activities that begin on the next page. These will help to prepare you for your work with the poem.

1. Write down the ideas that come into your head when you think of 'mushrooms'. You might comment on the following things.

   The colour of mushrooms.

   The shapes and sizes of mushrooms.

   The habits or 'behaviours' of mushrooms.

   The similarities between mushrooms and people.

   The lessons people could learn from mushrooms.

2. Share your notes with others in your group or class, and record the ideas on the board, or on a sheet of paper for each group.

Reading words

Sylvia Plath's poem, 'Mushrooms', can be read in at least two ways:

   a. as a description of the appearance and habits of mushrooms (for example, the way they spring up overnight);

   b. as an implied comparison between mushrooms and people (for example, the way apparently powerless people can triumph through persistence).

The words in Plath's poem have been chosen to emphasise a number of features about mushrooms. Some of these follow.

paleness	softness
silence	simplicity

The poem emphasises the apparent contradiction between the softness of mushrooms and their great persistence – their 'quiet strength'.

You will need to keep all of these ideas in mind as you read the poem.

Activities

   In the version of Sylvia Plath's poem on the following page a number of the words have been removed and a range of word choices placed alongside the text.

1. Read the poem and decide which *one* of the words in brackets you consider is the best choice to be used in that section of the poem. In making your decision, you will need to consider the sound and meanings or associations of each word, and how well each one fits with the ideas being developed in the poem. You may find it helpful to:

   – read the whole poem before working on each section;

   – read the poem aloud;

   – use the surrounding words as a guide when making your choices.

2. Compare your choices with those of others in your class, either in pairs or groups. Give reasons for the choices you have made. You can make changes to your choices if others offer a convincing argument.

3. When you have finished discussing your choices, refer to the end of the book (pages 151 and 152) to find Plath's original wording and to read the 'uninterrupted' poem.

MUSHROOMS

Overnight, very
Whitely, discreetly,
Very quietly

Our toes, our noses
Take hold on the loam,
_____ the air.   (Inhale/Acquire/Snatch)

Nobody sees us,
Stops us, _____ us,   (reveals/betrays/spots)
The small grains make room.

_____ fists insist on   (Strong/Soft/Spiky)
Heaving the needles,
The leafy bedding,

Even the paving.
Our hammers, our rams,
Earless and eyeless,

Perfectly _____ ,   (silent/voiceless/formed)
Widen the crannies,
Shoulder through holes. We

Diet on water,
On crumbs of _____ ,   (mould/shadow/moonlight)
Bland mannered, _____   (saying/asking/giving)

Little or nothing.
So many of us!
So many of us!

We are shelves, we are
Tables, we are _____ ,   (weak, meek, sleek)
We are edible,

_____ and shovers   (Rammers/Raiders/Nudgers)
In spite of ourselves.
Our kind multiplies:

We shall by morning
_____ the earth.   (Inherit/Take over/People)
Our foot's in the door.

Sylvia Plath

Reading verses

In the following activity you are asked to identify an original verse, or stanza, from alternatives that have been inserted in a poem. Two of the three alternative verses or stanzas of the poem that you are asked to read are 'fakes'. They differ slightly from the language and form of the original. As with the previous activity, you will need to consider the whole poem – its language, ideas and structure – when making your choice.

The poem you will read is 'The Earth Lover' by Australian poet Katharine Susannah Prichard.

Before going on to read the poem, work through the following activities. They will help to prepare you for your work with the poem.

Activities

1. Read carefully the following brief explanation of 'The Earth Lover' written by a student who has studied it.

> In "The Earth Lover" the speaker of the poem is asking to be allowed to lose her or himself in the beauty and richness of the earth. She wants to be enfolded in the earth's vegetation with all its greenery, its perfumes, its herbs and flowers, and its mosses. The speaker regards the earth as the source of life, and as the resting place in death, and she sees herself as deeply connected with the cycle of life on the earth. The poem can also be read as a request to be buried in the earth after she has died.

2. Based on this explanation, write down some of the expectations you have about Prichard's poem. You might find it helpful to begin by considering the following questions.

   a. What themes do you think the poem could explore?

   | Progress? | Life? | Gardening? |
   | Nature? | Death? | Religion? |

   b. What kind of language do you expect to find in the poem?

   | Plain language? | Mostly nouns? |
   | Very 'descriptive' language? | Mostly adjectives? |

   c. What kind of structure do you expect to find in the poem?

   | A strong rhyming pattern? | No rhyme? |
   | A regular rhythm? | Free verse? |

   d. What kind of poetic techniques do you expect to find?

   | Descriptions? | Images? |
   | Comparisons? | Symbols? |

3. The alternative versions of the third verse, only one of which was written by Katharine Susannah Prichard, are indented to the right of 'The Earth Lover' on the following page.

   Before trying to work out which is the original stanza or verse, read the whole poem through a number of times. Then go on to the activities that follow. These will help you to identify the stanza written by Katharine Susannah Prichard.

Studying Poetry   55

THE EARTH LOVER

Let me lie in the grass –
Bathe in its verdure
As one bathes in the sea –
Soul-drowned in herbage,
The essence of clover,
Dandelion, camomile, knapweed
And centaury.

Let me lie close to the earth,
Battened against the broad breast
Which brings all things to being
And gives rest to all things.

1. Let me restore the cycle of birth,
    Living, dying,
    Sweet mould in the earth,
    Renewing the life that quickly passes
    Amidst the heady herbal scent
    Of flowers, insects, weeds and grasses.

2. So will I escape the cycle of birth,
    Life and death,
    For decaying in the silent soil,
    Below the grasses, insects, herbs and flowers,
    I will rest in peace at last
    And leave the world behind.

3. Let me inspire the odours of birth,
    Death, living,
    Sweets of the mould,
    The generative sap of insects,
    Crushed in grasses, witch weeds,
    Flowering herbs.

For I am an earth child,
An earth lover,
And I ask no more than to be,
Of the earth, earthy,
And to mingle again with the divine dust.

Katharine Susannah Prichard

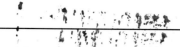

Remember: in thinking about your choice for Katharine Susannah Prichard's original stanza, you will need to consider the language and structure of the whole poem. One way of doing this is to summarise the ideas and images associated with each section of the poem.

1. The following is a summary of the first stanza of the poem. Read it carefully, then make your own summary of stanzas Two and Four.

Stanza One:

> **Form and language:**
> Free verse – not rhyming.
> First person point of view: 'Let *me* lie in the grass – '
> Lots of nouns related to vegetation, few adjectives or verbs.
> Old-fashioned words (verdure, herbage).
>
> **Main idea/statement:**
> Speaker wants to be enveloped by earth and its vegetation.
>
> **Notes:**
> 'Lie *in* the grass' (not *on* the grass) implies long, lush growth.
> (Could imply burial also).
> 'Bathes' and 'drowned' add to idea of being enveloped (or buried).
> Lots of different words for vegetation ('grass, verdure, herbage') build up impression of lushness through their number and repetition.
> List of plants gives a concrete image of the variety of plantlife.

Stanza Two:

> **Form and language:**
>
> **Main idea/statement:**
>
> **Notes:**

Stanza Four:

> **Form and language:**
>
> **Main idea/statement:**
>
> **Notes:**

2. Working on your own or with a partner, read through the three alternative versions of stanza 3. See if you can work out which is the original stanza by considering the statement or idea, and the form and use of language, in each.

3. Present your decision to the class or to your group by making a formal statement in which you state your choice and give clear reasons for your decision, eg:

   'I think number [   ] is the original stanza because _____ .'

   Give a clear explanation of at least two reasons for your choice, referring to the text to support your decision. (See page 153 for Katharine Susannah Prichard's original poem.)

POEMS WITHOUT WORDS?

Some poems seem to do away with words altogether. But even in these unusual poems we find that word *associations* are important in the reader's construction of meaning for the text.

'The Affair' by Alan Riddell is composed almost entirely of just two letters. Read the poem, then do the activities that follow it.

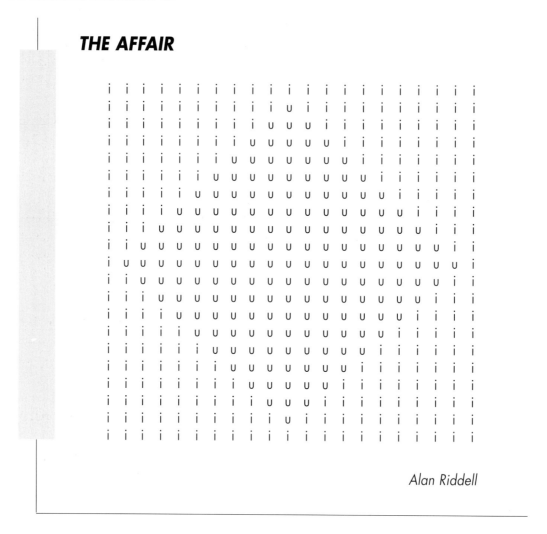

THE AFFAIR

Alan Riddell

Activities

1. When you have thought about the poem for a while, write a brief report of your reading.

   Note down:

   – *what* you think the poem is about, and
   – *how* you arrived at this reading.

2. Share your report with others in your group or class, and discuss the following points. What meanings have members of your group made from this text? What parts of the text did each person focus on? Was it:

   – the title?
   – the shape and pattern of the text?
   – the meanings of the letters?

   What information from 'outside' the text helped you make sense of the poem?

Constructing a reading

Below are the readings two students produced in response to this poem. They have explained what they thought the poem was saying and how they produced this reading. Compare these responses with how you read the poem.

1. I think the poem is about how relationships come and go, and how people can become obsessed by another person. At the beginning, in the first line, the person is totally wrapped up in herself, and the poem shows it by repeating "i, i, i ...". It is as if the poem is recording her thoughts or outlook on the world. In the second line it shows that she has met someone special and started to include him in her life and thoughts a little bit. The lines after that show how this other person becomes more and more important to her, until she is totally obsessed with him. Then gradually the affair fades out and she goes back to her normal life. I think it is a rather sad poem.

2. This poem is like a symbol for two people having an affair. The "u" pattern forms a diamond shape, which shows that the woman is loved dearly like a precious gem. The "i" letters are wrapped around the "u", showing how the lover tries to wrap his life around the other person. It also shows that the lover tries to hide her from others, because usually an affair is something that people try to keep secret. In this way the patterns show the ideas of love, protection and secrecy in an affair.

These two readings are significantly different from each other. This is partly because the two readers have approached the text in different ways.

Activity

Show which reader(s) used each of the following approaches to make sense of the poem.

Reading approach	Reader 1	Reader 2	Evidence
Treat the text as a story that develops over time.			
Treat the text as representing a moment in time, or an idea.			
Look for visual symbols in the text.			
Use the title as a guide to the meaning.			
Use past reading and experience to add background information.			

Readers' associations

Many readers use their knowledge about 'affairs' to add meaning to the text. The title of the poem seems to 'invite' us to do this. In fact, it is hard to see how readers could make sense of the poem if the title did not encourage them to draw on their 'background' knowledge or beliefs about 'affairs'.

This suggests that the way we read one text (such as a poem or story) is influenced by other texts we already know (other stories, and even our 'common sense' knowledge).

Activities

1. Consider the following ideas that were reported in the student readings above. Say which of them is 'in the text' and which seems to come from other stories and 'background' knowledge or beliefs about affairs, or is a combination of both.

Idea	Text	Background	Combination
The poet is a male.			
The 'i' is a male, the 'u' is a female.			
The 'i' is a female, the 'u' is a male.			
Affairs involve obsession.			
A chance meeting starts the affair.			
Affairs have a beginning, middle and end.			
The end of an affair is a sad occasion.			
An affair involves secrecy.			
An 'affair' means a love affair.			

2. Say which of the ideas above were also part of *your* reading of the poem. Where do you think these ideas might have come from?

3. Can this poem be read aloud? You could try to produce an individual, group or whole-class reading of Alan Riddell's poem, using the performance techniques you learned in Chapter One.

Conducting research

To test just how important a title can be in shaping a reading, you can conduct some research using this poem.

1. Show Alan Riddell's poem to three other people (you could choose friends, relations, or students in another class) *without the title*, and ask them the following questions.

   a. What do you think this poem might be about?
   b. Can you suggest a title for the poem?
   c. Which of the following do you think might be the title of the poem? (You could add other titles to these.)

   'The Enemy'   'The Affair'   'U and I'   'Loneliness'

2. Report back to your class with your findings. Compare the answers you received, and discuss what this information tells you about the importance of the title in shaping people's reading of the poem.

Other poems

1. Using Riddell's poem as a model, try writing other poems using only 'i' and 'u' that would fit the following titles. (You could assign one title to each person in your group.)

    'Rejection'   'Friends'
    'Obsession'   'Enemies'

2. Prepare neat copies of the poems to share – *without titles*. Then swap your poems with another group and see if they can correctly match the titles to each set of poems. When you have done this, discuss the following questions.

    a. Did readers always guess the 'correct' titles?
    b. If not, did they offer convincing arguments for their decisions?
    c. What kind of rules or reading practices did readers use in making sense of the texts?

    Were the following used:

    - matching the text to a common storyline about relationships?
    - comparing the number of 'i's and 'u's in the text?
    - reading visual patterns in the poem as symbols?
    - others?

Write a comparison

In working through this chapter you have seen that poems influence a reader's response through the selection and arrangement of words. This can be achieved in a variety of ways:

- through sound;
- through ideas and associations that they encourage;
- through the building-up of images, patterns and comparisons.

These are understandings that you can apply in your reading of all poems – and in writing about poetry.

On pages 62 and 63 are two different translations of a poem by French poet Jacques Prevert. His poem, which is presented as a set of instructions, could be described as an imaginative fantasy about the beauty of nature.

Like the translations, drafts and altered texts you have worked with in this chapter, these two versions of the poem use slightly different wordings.

Writing

Write a short critical discussion of the two versions of Jacques Prevert's poem, explaining which version you prefer and why. Refer back to Greg Allan's discussion on page 48 of 'First Frost' and 'First Ice' as a model for your own writing. You may also wish to look again at the suggestions, on pages 49–51, for writing an essay that compares two poems.

Some further suggestions for writing are provided *after* the two translations of Prevert's poem. To get you started, the following steps might be helpful.

1. Jot down your predictions about the subject and language of the poems from the titles.
2. Read the poems a number of times before starting your analysis.
3. Make notes about the sounds and associations of words by annotating or writing on your copy of the texts.

TO PAINT THE PORTRAIT OF A BIRD

First paint a cage
with an open door
then paint
something pretty
5 something simple
something beautiful
something useful ...
for the bird
then place the canvas against a tree
10 in a garden
in a wood
or in a forest
hide behind the tree
without speaking
15 without moving ...
Sometimes the bird comes quickly
but he can just as well spend long years
before deciding
Don't get discouraged
20 wait
wait years if necessary
the swiftness or slowness of the coming
of the bird having no rapport
with the success of the picture
25 When the bird comes
if he comes
observe the most profound silence
wait till the bird enters the cage
and when he has entered
30 gently close the door with a brush
then
paint out all the bars one by one
taking care not to touch any of the feathers of the bird
Then paint the portrait of the tree
35 choosing the most beautiful of its branches
for the bird
paint also the green foliage and the wind's freshness
the dust of the sun
and the noise of the insects in the summer heat
40 and then wait for the bird to decide to sing
If the bird doesn't sing
it's a bad sign
a sign that the painting is bad
but if he sings it's a good sign
45 a sign that you can sign
So then so very gently you pull out
one of the feathers of the bird
and you write your name in the corner of the picture.

Jacques Prevert
Trans. Lawrence Ferlinghetti

HOW TO PAINT THE PORTRAIT OF A BIRD

First paint a cage
with an open door
then paint
something pretty
5   something simple
something fine
something useful
for the bird
next place the canvas against a tree
10   in a garden
in a wood
or in a forest
hide behind the tree
without speaking
15   without moving ...
Sometimes the bird comes quickly
but it can also take many years
before making up its mind
Don't be discouraged
20   wait
wait if necessary for years
the quickness or the slowness of the coming
of the bird having no relation
to the success of the picture
25   When the bird comes
if it comes
observe the deepest silence
wait for the bird to enter the cage
and when it has entered
30   gently close the door with the paint-brush
then
one by one paint out all the bars
taking care not to touch one feather of the bird
Next make a portrait of the tree
35   choosing the finest of its branches
for the bird
paint also the green leaves and the freshness of the wind
dust in the sun
and the sound of the insects in the summer grass
40   and wait for the bird to decide to sing
If the bird does not sing
it is a bad sign
a sign that the picture is bad
but if it sings it is a good sign
45   a sign that you are ready to sign
so then you pluck very gently
one of the quills of the bird
and you write your name in the corner of the picture.

Jacques Prevert
Trans. Paul Dehn

Planning your essay

You may find it useful to organise your discussion of the two versions of Prevert's poem as follows. (You can use the brief examples as models to help structure your essay.)

1. Begin by outlining what you think the poem is about. You should try to state:

    – your 'first' or simple reading of the poem (a set of instructions? what about?);

    – the themes that you have read in the poem (is it a comment about art? about patience? about natural beauty?);

    – your reaction to the poem (contemplation? amusement?).

    Example:

    > Jacques Prevert's poem, entitled "To Paint the Portrait of a Bird" and "How to Paint the Portrait of a Bird" in the two translations, is obviously not meant to be taken seriously as a set of instructions for painting. Instead, it is an imaginative way of showing that ...

2. Discuss some of the differences in wording in the two versions, and say which translations you think are better, and why. In this section you should comment on such things as:

    – differences of sound (if relevant);

    – differences of meaning or associations (if relevant);

    – how these relate to the poem overall, as you read it.

    Example:

    > The two translations of Prevert's poem show how specific words and phrases can contribute to the overall effect of a text. One general difference between the texts is that the second version uses less common words in order to create a feeling of great seriousness. The use of "fine" rather than "beautiful" has the effect of ...

3. Conclude by stating which version of the poem you prefer overall, and say why.

    Example:

    > Taken as a whole, I believe that the more successful version of the poem is
    > ...
    > because
    > ...

Note how these three examples are structured: there is a *statement* about the poem or poems, which is then *explained* and *supported* by examples.

This could provide a useful model for you to follow. See pages 50–51 for a further reminder of how this essay and paragraph structure can work.

4.

Forms and Functions

YUH HEAR BOUT?

Yuh hear bout di people dem arres
Fi bun dung di Asian people dem house?
Yuh hear bout di policeman dem lock up
Fi beat up di black bwoy widout a cause?
Yuh hear bout di M.P. dem sack because im refuse fi help
im black constituents in a dem fight 'gainst deportation?
Yuh noh hear bout dem?
Me neida.

Valerie Bloom

BEYOND THE WORD

In Chapter Three you investigated how readers produce associations and responses for individual words and phrases in a poem. In this chapter you will learn about other aspects of poetry, such as the reading of metaphors, and responding to the form of a poem. You will also study the first drafts of some famous poems, to see how established forms and practices shape the writing and reading of poetry texts.

Making comparisons

A great deal of the language in many poems is devoted to description. Through description, poems attempt to offer the reader a representation of objects or ideas. Readers respond to these descriptions on the basis of their experiences, cultural backgrounds and reading contexts.

Sometimes poems describe things through direct statement like this:

The rain fell hard.

Other times the description may be achieved through various kinds of comparison, like this:

The raindrops fell like bullets.
or
The clouds unleashed an avalanche, pebbles of water that stung the skin.

In these lines we see one object (raindrops) being compared to another (bullets, pebbles).

Through such comparisons, the poem can invite the reader to make associations that will enhance the description. In this case the comparison activates ideas about violence, danger and injury. This is helpful if the poem is trying to create an image of ferocious weather. It might also help to develop an idea or argument – for example, the idea that nature can be harsh and cruel.

Simile, metaphor and personification are common kinds of comparison used. In this section you will focus on one kind of comparison – metaphor. You will see how metaphor can function in a poem, and you will learn how to use it in your own writing.

The following poem is famous for its use of vivid images, in particular its use of metaphor. It was written around 1905 by Alfred Noyes, a British poet. It tells of a highwayman (an outlaw on horseback) and his lover, Bess.

The poem has a strong rhythm and is most effective when read aloud. Read it through, then do the activities that follow.

THE HIGHWAYMAN

The wind was a torrent of darkness among the gusty trees,
The moon was a ghostly galleon tossed upon cloudy seas,
The road was a ribbon of moonlight over the purple moor,
And the highwayman came riding –
    Riding – riding –
The highwayman came riding, up to the old inn door.

He'd a French-cocked hat on his forehead, a bunch of lace at his chin,
A coat of the claret velvet, and breeches of brown doeskin;
They fitted with never a wrinkle: his boots were up to the thigh!
And he rode with a jewelled twinkle,
    His pistol butts a-twinkle,
His rapier hilt a-twinkle, under the jewelled sky.

Over the cobbles he clattered and clashed in the dark inn-yard,
And he tapped with his whip on the shutters, but all was locked and barred;
He whistled a tune to the window, and who should be waiting there
But the landlord's black-eyed daughter,
    Bess, the landlord's daughter,
Plaiting a dark red love-knot into her long black hair.

And dark in the dark old inn-yard a stable wicket creaked
Where Tim the ostler listened; his face was white and peaked;
His eyes were hollows of madness, his hair like mouldy hay,
But he loved the landlord's daughter,
    The landlord's red-lipped daughter,
Dumb as a dog he listened, and he heard the robber say –

"One kiss, my bonny sweetheart, I'm after a prize tonight,
But I shall be back with the yellow gold before the morning light;
Yet if they press me sharply, and harry me through the day,
Then look for me by moonlight,
    Watch for me by moonlight,
I'll come to thee by moonlight, though hell should bar the way."

He rose upright in the stirrups: he scarce could reach her hand,
But she loosed her hair i' the casement! His face burnt like a brand
As the black cascade of perfume came tumbling over his breast;
And he kissed its waves in the moonlight,
    (Oh, sweet black waves in the moonlight!)
Then he tugged at his rein in the moonlight, and galloped away to the west.

II

He did not come in the dawning; he did not come at noon;
And out o' the tawny sunset, before the rise o' the moon,
When the road was a gypsy's ribbon, looping the purple moor,
A red-coat troop came marching –
    Marching, – marching –
King George's men came marching, up to the old inn-door.

They said no word to the landlord, they drank his ale instead,
But they gagged his daughter and bound her to the foot of her narrow bed,
Two of them knelt at her casement, with muskets at their side!
There was death at every window;
    And hell at one dark window;
For Bess could see, through her casement, the road that *he* would ride.

They had tied her up to attention, with many a sniggering jest;
They had bound a musket beside her, with the muzzle beneath her breast!
"Now keep good watch!" and they kissed her. She heard the dead man say –
Look for me by moonlight;
    Watch for me by moonlight;
I'll come to thee by moonlight, though hell should bar the way!

She twisted her hands behind her; but all the knots held good!
She writhed her hands till her fingers were wet with sweat or blood!
They stretched and strained in the darkness, and the hours crawled by like years,
Till, now, on the stroke of midnight,
    Cold, on the stroke of midnight,
The tip of one finger touched it! The trigger at least was hers!

The tip of one finger touched it; she strove no more for the rest!
Up, she stood up to attention, with the muzzle beneath her breast.
She would not risk their hearing; she would not strive again;
For the road lay bare in the moonlight;
　　Blank and bare in the moonlight;
And the blood of her veins, in the moonlight, throbbed to her love's refrain.

Tlot-tlot; tlot-tlot! Had they heard it? The horse-hoofs ringing clear;
Tlot-tlot; tlot-tlot, in the distance? Were they deaf that they did not hear?
Down the ribbon of moonlight, over the brow of the hill,
The highwayman came riding,
　　Riding, riding!
The red-coats looked to their priming! She stood up straight and still!

Tlot-tlot in the frosty silence! *Tlot-tlot* in the echoing night!
Nearer he came and nearer! Her face was like a light!
Her eyes grew wide for a moment; she drew one last deep breath,
Then her finger moved in the moonlight,
　　Her musket shattered the moonlight,
Shattered her breast in the moonlight, and warned him with her death.

He turned; he spurred to the westward; he did not know who stood
Bowed, with her head o'er the musket, drenched with her own red blood!
Not till the dawn he heard it, and slowly blanched to hear,
How Bess, the landlord's daughter,
　　The landlord's black-eyed daughter,
Had watched for her love in the moonlight, and died in the darkness there.

Back he spurred like a madman, shouting a curse to the sky,
With the white road smoking behind him and his rapier brandished high!
Blood-red were his spurs i' the golden noon; wine-red was his velvet coat;
When they shot him down on the highway,
　　Down like a dog on the highway,
And he lay in his blood on the highway, with a bunch of lace at his throat.

And still of a winter's night, they say, when the wind is in the trees,
When the moon is a ghostly galleon tossed upon cloudy seas,
When the road is a ribbon of moonlight over the purple moor,
A highwayman comes riding –
　　Riding – riding –
A highwayman comes riding, up to the old inn-door.

Over the cobbles he clatters and clangs in the dark inn-yard,
He taps with his whip on the shutters, but all is locked and barred;
He whistles a tune to the window, and who should be waiting there
But the landlord's black-eyed daughter,
　　Bess, the landlord's daughter,
Plaiting a dark-red love knot into her long black hair.

Alfred Noyes

'The Highwayman' offers the reader many strong images. Images are descriptions that readers find powerful, and which may evoke a strong response from the reader, such as a 'mental picture' and a feeling of atmosphere.

1. List some of the images that you can find in 'The Highwayman'. Below are two examples to get you started. Add another six to the list.

    Images: **1.** the wind in the trees   5. _____
             2. the moon in the cloudy sky   6. _____
             3. _____   7. _____
             4. _____   8. _____

2. Now decide which of these images you find most effective.

Metaphor as description

A *metaphor* is a form of comparison in which one object or idea is described in terms of another object or idea. In this way, the first object 'takes on' certain qualities that the reader would normally associate with the second.

In the example below, a familiar 'object' – rain, is portrayed as something else – a fall of rocks:

> **The clouds unleashed an avalanche, pebbles of water that stung the skin.**

The same technique is used in 'The Highwayman':

> **The moon was a ghostly galleon tossed upon cloudy seas.**

In this metaphor, a familiar 'object' – the moon, is described as something else – a kind of sailing ship (a galleon).

1. Readers may have a number of *associations* for the image of a 'ghostly galleon', such as those listed below.

    The bobbing movement of a ship on the ocean.   ☐

    Stories of adventure and danger.   ☐

    Ideas about shipping, trade and commerce.   ☐

    The physical appearance of a boat.   ☐

    The foaming of waves as a ship ploughs through them.   ☐

    Treasure chests and pieces of eight.   ☐

    Pirates and smugglers.   ☐

    Which of these associations seem to you to be most relevant to the poem? Rank the items from 1 (most relevant) to 7 (least relevant).

2. Compare your rankings with others in your class, and discuss how the associations add to the effectiveness of the poem.

3. Lines 1 and 3 in verse 1 of 'The Highwayman' (on page 66) also contain metaphors. For each line, note down the following.

    The *object* being described.   _____

    The *comparison* being made.   _____

    The *associations* triggered by the comparison.   _____

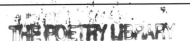

Reading metaphors

In order to make sense of poems that contain metaphors, readers have to supply the background information that makes the comparison 'work'. In making these associations or connections, the reader is led to think more actively about the idea.

Following is one reader's explanation of the metaphor below.

Metaphor:

> **We waited, while the politicians preened themselves and strutted importantly back and forth.**

Explanation:

> This metaphor compares the politicians to a flock of birds. I get an impression of them as pigeons, which are sometimes pompous-looking, even though they aren't particularly bright. Describing politicians in this ways sets up a contrast between the common idea of politicians as important people, and the image of them as unthinking, small-minded and not very important in the grand scheme of things. The comparison makes a comment about politicians without coming right out and saying it.

Activity

1. Write your own brief explanations of the following metaphors.

   > **All the world's a stage and all the men and women merely players; they have their entrances and their exits.**

   > **Their love was a fire that had flared quickly and burned hot, but only the glowing embers remained. Soon it would be cold.**

2. Compare your explanations with those of others in your class or group.

Criteria for judging metaphors

The effectiveness of a particular metaphor may depend upon many factors, including:

- how well it fits in with the language and ideas of the text;
- how well it fits the cultural background, values and attitudes of the reader.

Some criteria that readers can use to judge the effectiveness of a metaphor are listed below.

Sound	The wording of a metaphor may assist the description by suggesting a particular mood or tone.
Associations	The objects or actions may activate associations that help or hinder the comparison.
Visual imagery	The comparison may help readers construct a mental image.
Freshness or surprise	Often a comparison will offer a new way of looking at or thinking about the object.
Familiarity	Sometimes the value of a metaphor lies in its familiarity.

1. In the commentaries below, two students have used these criteria to judge a metaphor. Read through the commentary that follows each metaphor and see if you agree with it.

The sun was a fat-fried egg in the clear blue sky.

I don't think this one works. There's a visual similarity between the sun and the fried egg – both are yellow and round, and sky around the sun is often very pale – almost white, so it almost works as an image. It has the value of being surprising, too. But I think the associations of sun and fried egg are wrong. People usually think of the sun as pure and clean, but frying in fat is unhealthy and smelly. Also, the phrase "clear blue sky" seems out of place. Like the sun, it seems clean and pure. It might work better if the sky was described differently: "The sun was a fat-fried egg in the sizzling air." But this still isn't great. I would try to think of a different comparison.

– Tan

The sky was a solid mass of cloud,
a blue-white Arctic sea
that flowed upside down to the horizon,
where the sun shone pale and distant.

Comparing a cloudy sky to a sea full of ice and snow is effective, I think. It gave me the impression of coldness, a very slow movement, and a feeling that the cloud stretched on forever. The visual image and the associations are the best points here. I am not sure about the wording. The third and fourth lines seem a bit too wordy. I don't think the phrase "upside down" is really needed. I think readers could be left to make that connection for themselves. But overall I think this is quite a good metaphor.

– Gemma

2. Your turn: Below are listed three common objects or events. They are followed by alternative metaphoric descriptions.

Read through them and then do the activities that follow.

1. A smashed car windscreen.

   a. The cracked glaze of ancient porcelain.
   b. A layer of crystal honeycomb.
   c. Crushed ice spilled onto the road.

2. Winter fog around city skyscrapers.

   a. A thick blanket of fog settled on the city.
   b. A soft white tide swept in and flowed around the buildings.
   c. A river of mist flowed past skyscraper pylons.

3. Pigeons roosting on a powerline.

   a. Fluffy notes on a clothesline staff.
   b. Fuzzy knots on cat's cradle wires.
   c. Dull beads threaded on a taut black string.

3. Give each of the alternative metaphors a rating, using this three-point scale:

1 = Very effective
2 = Acceptable
3 = Not effective

For each rating, give a brief explanation for your decision set out as below. (Consider the criteria for judging a metaphor listed on page 70 when making your evaluations.)

Metaphor	Rating	Explanation
1 (a) 1 (b) 1 (c)		
2 (a) 2 (b) 2 (c)		
3 (a) 3 (b) 3 (c)		

4. Compare your ratings in a class or group discussion.

Writing metaphors

Writing effective metaphors is a complex but interesting task. It requires you to think about:

- the object you are trying to describe;
- the associations or connections you want your reader to make.

The three-step approach shown below can be helpful. Start by drawing three columns on your page, then do the following.

1. Think about the object or event you want to describe. Write down a list of *qualities* of the object that you want to emphasise. Put this information into column 1.
2. In your second column, list objects or ideas that you *associate* with the items in column 1.
3. In the third column, write down some qualities and associations for selected items in column 2.

This activity helps to stretch your thinking by creating a chain of associations. You can see how the process works in the example set out in the table below.

Object: a cloudy sky in winter

1 Qualities of object	2 Associations for column 1	3 Associations for column 2
cold grey vast dull depressing	cold = ice, winter, Antarctica, penguins, jumper grey = old, dull, boring, government buildings, battleship, sea vast = desert, space, cold, distant	Antarctica = snow, glacier, ice floe, empty government = vast, slow, irresistible, mindless

Once the associations have been mapped out, the metaphor can be constructed by drawing on ideas from the table. You should find there are associations and comparisons in the table that you would not normally have thought about.

The final stage is to experiment with different ideas and different ways of wording your metaphor, and to then choose the one that works best. For example:

> **The sky was a floe of Antarctic ice.**
> **The sky was a solid mass of cloud, a blue-white Antarctic sea.**
> **Grey government-issue clouds, slow and irresistible bureaucracies of mist.**

Activities

1. Use the three-step method to write metaphors for objects or events that are familiar to you. You could choose your topics from the following list, or work from your own ideas.

Waves breaking on a reef.	A row of terrace houses.
A line of cars on a busy freeway.	The wind rushing through powerlines.
A cloudless night sky.	A winter sunset.

2. Present your metaphors to your group or class, and discuss their effectiveness.

Metaphors in context

You can use metaphors in your own writing to help shape the way readers will respond. One way of doing this is to use an existing poem as a model.

'The Highwayman' provides a ready-made structure for using metaphors in a narrative poem. It can be adapted to suit other historic or fictional characters and events that you know of.

In this example, the structure of Noyes' poem has been used to plan a poem about the Australian bushranger Ned Kelly and his gang. Blank spaces in the poem show where the metaphors – for describing sun, heat and road in an Australian setting – need to be inserted.

THE HIGHWAYMAN

The wind was a torrent of darkness among the gusty trees,
The moon was a ghostly galleon tossed upon cloudy seas,
The road was a ribbon of moonlight over the purple moor,
And the highwayman came riding –
    Riding – riding –
The highwayman came riding, up to the old inn door.

THE KELLY GANG

The sun was a _____ ,
The heat was _____ ,
The road was _____ over the red-dust plain,
And the Kelly Gang came riding –
    Riding – riding –
The Kelly Gang came riding, up to the bank again.

Writing

You could try writing metaphors for 'The Kelly Gang', or create your own poem using this pattern, by working through the activities on the next page.

Activities

1. Choose a set of characters and events that could serve as the basis for your poem. The following are possibilities to consider.

    The Clantons, a famous outlaw gang from the American west, who fought in the shoot-out at the OK corral. (The Clantons came a-riding – riding – riding ...)

    > Robin Hood and his Merry Men, outlaw figures from British folk tales who fought against the Normans in England. (The Merry Men came riding – riding – riding ...)

    The suffragettes, women who protested for voting rights in Britain in the early 1900s. (The suffragettes came marching – marching – marching ...)

    > Civil rights campaigners who fought for African-American equality in the United States. (The people came forth singing – singing – singing ...)

    Yagan, an Aboriginal Australian who struggled against the whites on behalf of his people. (He faced the whites proudly – proudly – proudly ...)

    In planning your opening stanzas, you might find it helpful to do the following.

    1. Find out a little bit about the characters and events involved in the story.
    2. List some features of the setting that will help readers imagine the scene.
    3. Decide on the tone or mood that is appropriate to your subject (humorous, respectful, dignified etc.)
    4. Design metaphors to match your chosen subject matter and the rhythms of the poem.
    5. Give your poem a title that will alert your readers to the subject.
    6. Use the pattern of 'The Highwayman' and 'The Kelly Gang' to write your poem.

    Remember: Your language and comparisons should attempt to guide your readers to respond in the way that you think is appropriate.

2. These poems could be delivered to your group or class as oral presentations. Prepare your reading carefully, making sure to introduce the poem and the topic.

3. Other class or group members can provide feedback on your poem by filling in a response sheet like the one below. You could use the comments as a guide for redrafting your poem.

AUDIENCE RESPONSE SHEET
PRESENTER: _____
POEM TITLE: _____
1. Note down one metaphoric description that you found effective in the poem.
2. Briefly say why you found the description effective.
3. Note down one metaphoric description that you think could be improved.
4. Briefly say why you found this description less effective, and how it could be improved.
5. Note down any other relevant comments.

PATTERNS IN POETRY

Poetry achieves its effects through more than words and ideas. The words in a poem are always arranged within a particular *form* – a pattern or structure that guides the reading and writing of the poem. A poem's form can be established through rhyming patterns, rhythms, or the arrangement of lines. Some forms, such as the sonnet, have a wide usage and a long history. Others may be developed within a single poem or group of poems.

Form is one of the important elements of poetry that writers and readers jointly rely on when making their meanings. Readers often will have expectations about particular forms, such as the kind of subject that the poem will deal with. Poets take account of these expectations, even if their aim is to challenge them.

On the next page you will find a range of poems representing different poetic forms.

Activity

1. Working on your own, or with a partner, examine the poems and group them into categories on the basis of their forms.

2. For each category, list the features that are *shared* by the poems, such as the:

    – number of lines in the poem;
    – layout;
    – use of rhyme;
    – use of rhythm;
    – use of imagery.

3. Having placed the poems in categories on the basis of their forms and listed their features, see if you can give a name to the form.

Some names of forms and brief definitions follow to help you decide.

Sonnet	A poem written in 14 lines of 5 beats, usually exploring a feeling or state of mind rather than telling a story.
Haiku	A short poem presenting images of nature, with no strong rhythm or rhyme.
Ballad	A traditional folk-song that tells a story, in four line stanzas with a regular rhythm and rhyme.
Cinquain	A short poem of five unrhymed lines.
Heroic couplets	A poem in rhyming pairs of lines, with five beats per line, often telling a story.
Limerick	A humorous poem of five lines with a strict rhyme and rhythm.
Villanelle	A poem of five three line stanzas using only two rhymes, repeated throughout.
Ode	A lyric poem usually addressed to a particular subject, with lines of varying lengths and complex rhythms.

(The answers are printed on page 151)

1.

Since there's no help, come let us kiss and part;
Nay, I have done, you get no more of me,
And I am glad, yea, glad with all my heart
That thus so cleanly I myself can free.
Shake hands forever; cancel all our vows,
And, when we meet at any time again,
Be it not seen in either of our brows
That we one jot of former love retain.
Now at the last gasp of Love's latest breath,
When, his pulse failing, Passion speechless lies,
When Faith is kneeling by his bed of death,
And Innocence is closing up his eyes,
Now if thou wouldst, when all have given him over,
From death to life thou mightst him yet recover.

2.

Just now,
Out of the strange
Still dusk ... as strange as still
A white moth flew.
Why am I grown so cold?

3.

Night – and once again,
while I wait for you, cold wind
turns into rain.

4.

There was a knight, a most distinguished man,
Who from the moment that he first began
To ride abroad had followed chivalry,
Truth, honour, generousness and courtesy.
He had done nobly in his sovereign's war
And ridden into battle, no man more,
As well in Christian as in heathen places
And ever honoured for his noble graces.
He was of sovereign value in all eyes,
And though so much distinguished he was wise
And in his bearing modest as a maid.
He never yet a boorish thing had said
In all his life to any, come what might;
He was a true and perfect gentle-knight.

5.

What dire offense from amorous causes springs,
What mighty contests rise from trivial things,
I sing! This verse to Caryll, muse, is due:
This even Belinda may vouchsafe to view:
Slight is the subject, but not so the praise,
If she inspire and he approve my lays.
Say, what strange motive, goddess, could compel
A well-bred lord to assault a gentle belle?
Oh, say what stranger cause, yet unexplored,
Could make a gentle belle reject a lord?

6.

Bright the full moon shines.
On the matting on the floor –
Shadows of the pines.

7.

These be
Three silent things:
The falling snow ... the hour
Before the dawn ... the mouth of one
Just dead.

8.

Death, be not proud, though some have called thee
Mighty and dreadful, for thou art not so;
For those whom thou thinks't thou dost overthrow
Die not, poor Death, nor yet canst thou kill me.
From rest and sleep, which but thy pictures be,
Much pleasure; then from thee, much more must flow,
And soonest our best men with thee do go,
Rest of their bones, and souls' delivery.
Thou art slave to fate, chance, kings, and desperate men,
And dost with poison, war and sickness dwell,
And poppy or charms can make us sleep as well
And better than thy stroke; why swell'st thou then?
One short sleep past, we wake eternally
And death shall be no more; Death, thou shalt die.

Forms as genres

The form of a poem is more than just a convenient structure. In the eyes of readers, a poem's form links it to a whole tradition of usage. The poem becomes a member of a category, or *genre*, of poetry. In this way, the form of a poem can trigger a range of reader expectations, and so shape the way a poem is read.

Looking at form: haiku

Studying a simple form such as the haiku can reveal a lot about the way form influences the reading and writing of poetry.

Haiku is a form of poetry that originated in Japan. Influential haiku poets include Matsuo Basho, Kobayashi Issa and Masaoka Shiki. In their original form, haiku were the introductory verses of longer poems called *tanka*, but they have become popular as a form in their own right since the seventeenth century.

The following are translations of some traditional haiku. Read them through, then do the activities that follow.

HAIKU

1. On a withered branch
   a crow has settled –
   Autumn nightfall.
   Basho

2. Though it be broken –
   Broken again – still it's there:
   The moon on the water.
   Choshu

3. Bright the full moon shines.
   On the matting on the floor –
   Shadows of the pines.
   Kikaku

4. In unending rain
   The house-pent boy is fretting
   With his brand new kite.
   Shoha

5. There a beggar goes
   Heaven and earth he's wearing
   For his summer clothes.
   Kikaku

6. A storm wind blows –
   Out from among the grasses
   The full moon grows.
   Chora

7. On a leaf, a leaf
   Is casting a green shadow
   And the tree frog sings!
   Anonymous

---

1. To help focus your reading of the poems, try to give each haiku a title that captures the subject of the poem. List your titles as below.

   1 _____ 2 _____

   3 _____ 4 _____

   5 _____ 6 _____

                  7 _____

2. Before reading on, try to work out the *features* of the haiku form, using the poems on page 77 as a guide. Write your answers down. You should consider such things as:

   – subject matter;
   – structure of ideas;
   – layout.

   You may find it useful to work with a partner.

A simple form?

The haiku form is deceptive. It has a number of strict requirements that make the writing of good haiku quite demanding. These are the key features of the form.

1. A seventeen syllable structure, organised as follows:

   First line –   5 syllables (In / un / en- / ding / rain)
   Second line – 7 syllables (The / house / pent / boy / is / fret- / ting)
   Third line –   5 syllables (With / his / brand / new / kite)

2. A traditional subject matter emphasising nature and the seasons, and how the seasons affect human lives.

3. An emphasis on images rather than explanation.

4. A structure of ideas based on a one-line image, and a two-line image.

5. A shift in the scale of the images, from a large scale image (the world, or natural forces) to a small scale image (a part of the world, a person or object), or *vice-versa*.

Go back to the haiku you have read and see how they conform to these features. (You will notice that some haiku break one or more of the conventions.)

Write a haiku

Try writing your own haiku poem. Choose a season to represent, and try to convey your feelings about it through a pair of images. Base your images on aspects of the natural environment where you live.

As starting points for images, you might find linking the two ideas in each line below useful.

    a cloudy sky / a single ray of sunshine
    heat haze on the sand / cool ocean waves
    wind in the trees / a falling leaf

Reader expectations

You now know quite a lot about the haiku form. This knowledge may make you a more effective reader of haiku in future, because you will have a firm set of expectations about the genre. In short, you will know what to read or look for.

This familiarity makes it possible for new haiku either to confirm or challenge your expectations. In this way, the *genre* provides a framework within which both the reader and the writer must work.

With this in mind, read the following haiku.

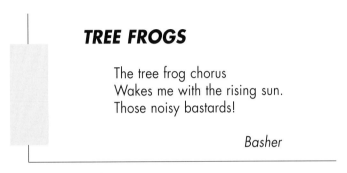

TREE FROGS

The tree frog chorus
Wakes me with the rising sun.
Those noisy bastards!

Basher

Discussion

1. In what ways, if any, did this haiku surprise you? Would all readers find the poem amusing, or are there aspects to the joke that require the reader to have some knowledge of conventional haiku? You might find it useful to list the ways this poem plays with the traditional haiku form.

2. What does this activity reveal about the relationship between form and reader expectations?

3. Do expectations apply only to specific forms of poetry? Or do readers have expectations about 'poetry in general'?

The social dimension

The haiku is a very popular form in Japan. Many people are enthusiastic readers and writers of haiku. This means that readers and writers share a strong set of expectations.

In Japan, the writing and reading of haiku is not merely a 'literary' or 'artistic' pursuit. It is also linked to broader cultural beliefs and practices – for example, a cultural life that is strongly linked to the passage of the seasons. This reminds us that forms of poetry are socially and culturally specific.

Even though you have learned the features of haiku, you still may not produce the same 'response' as a Japanese reader. Haiku often seem bland to modern Western readers, who tend to prefer narrative, or a strong sense of a speaker's voice. This suggests that our responses (which we like to see as personal) are strongly shaped by our cultural values and our training as readers.

Readers can benefit from learning something about the social and cultural origins of particular poems and forms of poetry. But this knowledge does not guarantee that the reader will make the same meaning from a poem that was intended by the poet.

Looking at form: the sonnet

The sonnet has been an important form in the history of English poetry. It originated in Italy and spread to England in the sixteenth century. It was taken up by many poets, including John Milton, William Shakespeare, Elizabeth Barrett Browning and William Wordsworth. There are a number of variations on the form, but certain features remain fairly constant.

Activities

1. Working with a partner, make a list of the formal features of a sonnet. Poems 1 and 8 on page 76 are sonnets, as is the poem by Shakespeare below. Use the following headings to guide your note-making.

   1. Length.
   2. Rhyming pattern.
   3. Rhythm.
   4. Typical ideas or content.
   5. Language.
   6. Development and arrangement of ideas.

2. Share your findings with others, and add new features to your list. As you work through this section, you will find out more about the features of the sonnet form.

A Shakespearian sonnet

The following well-known sonnet is by William Shakespeare. It was written around 1609. It is sometimes referred to as 'Shall I Compare Thee?'

Read the poem, then do the activities that follow.

SONNET 18

1   Shall I compare thee to a summer's day?
Thou art more lovely and more temperate:
Rough winds do shake the darling buds of May,
4   And summer's lease hath all too short a date.
Sometimes too hot the eye of heaven shines,
And often is his gold complexion dimmed;
And every fair from fair sometime declines
8   By chance or nature's changing course untrimmed.
But thy eternal summer shall not fade,
Nor lose possession of that fair thou ow'st,
Nor shall death brag thou wander'st in his shade
12   When in eternal lines to time thou grow'st.
So long as men can breathe or eyes can see
14   So long lives this, and this gives life to thee.

William Shakespeare

The speaker in this poem is addressing the lines to a particular person – perhaps a lover. The language of the poem can seem old fashioned to modern readers, and this can make it hard to follow.

Activity

1. Printed below is a paraphrase of Sonnet 18 in modern English – but the lines have been jumbled. Reconstruct the paraphrase by numbering the lines in the correct order, from 1 to 14. You will need to refer back to the original poem on the previous page to do this, and this will help you to make sense of the text.

The first line has been numbered for you.

	In summer, there are strong winds that shake the flowers
	Summer is only with us for a short time
	You are more beautiful and less harsh
	By accident, or through the passing of time, beauty is lost
	You won't lose the loveliness that you have
1	Shall I compare you to a day in summer
	All beautiful things eventually lose their attractiveness
	Your beauty is recorded in print forever
	For as long as civilisation survives
	This poem will keep your memory alive
	Even death can't cast a shadow over your beauty
	Sometimes the sun is too hot for comfort
	Other times it is cloudy and dull
	Your attractiveness will not be lost, however

2. Check your numbering with a partner.

The sonnet's structure

The ideas in a sonnet are often developed in stages, with each stage introducing a different aspect of the overall argument. We can summarise the 'idea-structure' of Shakespeare's sonnet like this:

Idea 1 (lines 1–4)	Shall I compare you to a day in summer? But you are more beautiful, and summer is not always pleasant, so that comparison won't work.
Idea 2 (lines 5–8)	Nothing on earth is permanent, so why should I compare your beauty to things that won't last?
Idea 3 (lines 9–12)	I won't compare you to things that will fade. I will preserve your memory in writing.
Idea 4 (lines 13–14)	You will live on forever, in my poem – because it will be read forever.

The sonnet develops its ideas in three *quatrains* (groups of four lines), followed by a *couplet* (two lines) that concludes the argument.

Go back and read the sonnet again, with this structure in mind.

Conventions

In the sixteenth century, the sonnet form was highly conventionalised. Sonnets not only had a strict form; they had a common function, or use. Sonnets were often written for the purpose of praising or complimenting someone – just as nowadays people might give a Valentine's Day gift or card. Poets sometimes wrote sonnets to flatter someone who might be able to offer them employment or patronage (for example, a member of royalty).

The content and methods of the sonnet were also conventional. Typically, the poems made flattering comparisons between the beauties of nature and the qualities of the favoured person. When we read Shakespeare's Sonnet 18 in this light, we can see that it *twists* some of these conventions.

Discussion

How does the argument of Sonnet 18 twist the conventions of praise and flattery? Find ways in which the poem seems to break with convention. Discuss these points in your group.

Rhythm in a sonnet

Sonnets are typically written in *iambic pentameter* – a rhythm in which there are five strong beats per line, in this pattern:

$$\cup \,/\, \mid \cup \,/\, \mid \cup \,/\, \mid \cup \,/\, \mid \cup \,/$$

Shall I | compare | thee to | a sum | mer's day

'Penta - meter' means 'five - beats', and an iambus is a rhythmical unit – called a *foot* – in which there is one unstressed syllable followed by one stressed syllable. Readers need to be aware of this rhythmical structure, especially if the poem is to be read aloud. The quality of the rhythm is one of the measures often used to judge the success of a sonnet.

Activities

1. Some of the following lines are in iambic pentameter; others are not. Working with a partner, read the lines aloud to each other and make a note of those that you think *are* in iambic pentameter.

    a. There was a man who lived in London town.
    b. A froggie went a-courting on a summer's day.
    c. The sea is calm tonight, the tide is high.
    d. Do not go gentle into that good night.
    e. Black was the night and the stars were afire.
    f. There was a young man from Peru.

2. Choose one of the lines you have decided is in iambic pentameter and try to mark in the stress pattern, as in the example above. You can underline the stressed syllables, or mark them with a slash above the stress. (Both have been done in the example above.)

3. Re-write the following lines so that they fit the iambic pentameter pattern. You may need to add or delete words or syllables.

    a. I met a trav'ller from a far land.
    b. The miller was a very large and brawny man.

4. Write endings for the following lines, so that the line is in iambic pentameter.

    a. My lover's eyes _____
    b. He thought he saw _____
    c. The autumn leaves _____

Missing lines

You can test your understanding of the sonnet form by filling in the missing sections of an existing poem.

In this activity you will work with another sonnet by Shakespeare: Sonnet 130 which is sometimes referred to as 'My Mistress's Eyes'.

Like Sonnet 18 on page 80, Sonnet 130 also twists some of the conventions of the typical sonnet. It begins by pointing out that many of the flattering comparisons made in sonnets are not really believable.

Before you read the sonnet, study its idea-structure, as set out below.

Idea 1   My mistress doesn't have eyes like sunshine, or lips like red coral.
Her hair is not soft and her skin is not white as snow.

Idea 2   I know what flowers look like, and how they smell –
and my mistress doesn't look or smell like that.

Idea 3   Her voice doesn't sound like music, and she doesn't walk
like a goddess. She is much more real.

Idea 4   But I think she is as beautiful as any woman who has
been flattered with these false comparisons.

The Sonnet itself is printed below. Two lines have been deleted. Read the poem carefully, and refer back to the summary above to check your understanding of the argument.

SONNET 130

1   My mistress' eyes are nothing like the sun;
Coral is far more red than her lips' red;
If snow be white, why then her breasts are dun;   (dun = dull brown)
4   If hairs be wires, black wires grow on her head.
I have seen roses damasked red and white,   (damasked = dappled)
But no such roses see I in her cheeks;
And in some perfumes is there more delight
8   Than (1. _____)
I love to hear her speak, but well I know
That (2. _____)
I grant I never saw a goddess go,
12   My mistress when she walks, treads on the ground.
And yet, by heaven, I think my love as rare
14   As any she belied with false compare.   (belied = misrepresented)

William Shakespeare

The task here is to write your own lines to fill the gaps in 'Sonnet 130' on the previous page.

To do this, you will need to think carefully about:

   – the ideas being developed in the poem;
   – the rhyming pattern;
   – the rhythmical pattern.

1. Start by working out which lines the missing sections must *rhyme* with. You can do this by referring to the following outline. Lines which rhyme are labelled with the same letter of the alphabet. (You could transfer these rhyme labels to the poem.)

   _____ a
   _____ b
   _____ a
   _____ b
   _____ c
   _____ d
   _____ c
   _____ d
   _____ e
   _____ f
   _____ e
   _____ f
   _____ g
   _____ g

2. Now write lines that help develop the ideas in the poem. Here are clues about the content of the missing lines:

   – the first missing line describes the woman's breath;
   – the second missing line refers to music.

Make sure that your lines follow the iambic pentameter pattern in the poem.

3. When you have written your lines, compare your efforts with a partner. (The original lines are printed on page 151.)

Write a sonnet

The sonnet is a complex form, but you can learn to write one using the knowledge you have of its structure and by following Shakespeare's example.

Your sonnet can be written in modern English, but it should conform to the basic sonnet conventions:

   – a 14 line poem of praise or honour;
   – an argument developed in stages;
   – a set rhyme (typically an 'abab cdcd efef gg' pattern);
   – a set rhythm (five stressed beats per line, called iambic pentameter).

On the next page is a sonnet written by a student, using the Shakespearian sonnet as a model. The sonnet has been written in praise of the country Australia.

MY COUNTRY

'The Lucky Country' some have called this land,
With forest green and desert painted red,
Ringed by ocean blue and creamy sand,
With crystal skies and bright stars overhead.
It can be harsh at times, and unforgiving,
With dangers that can tax the bravest heart;
But through it all, there is a joy of living,
A spiritual bond that can't be torn apart.
And yet there is a dark side to this nation,
A history that's tainted still with shame,
Of how the first inhabitants were treated
When first the settlers to this country came.
But with the riches that we have to share
Our common future still can be so fair.

Annette Ross

Activity

1. Some lines in Annette Ross's sonnet still need polishing. List examples of the following, and discuss them with your group.

   Places where the rhythm or sound is not smooth enough.
   Places where the expression of the ideas is awkward.

   You could try repairing these sections of the poem with minor re-writing.

2. Your turn: Annette Ross worked through *three* stages to produce her poem. You may find it useful to use the same steps to write your own sonnet.

   Step 1.
   Choose a topic that invites praise: a place, a person, or other subject. The following are some topics you could choose to write about.

   Your country, state or suburb.
   Your favourite sports team.
   Your school.
   A person you admire or respect.

   Step 2.
   Second, develop a simple argument, in three or four stages.

   Here is the outline Annette Ross created for her sonnet. Compare this intended structure with the final version of her poem, printed above.

Idea 1	My country is known for its natural beauty.
Idea 2	It is also a harsh land, with many challenges.
Idea 3	It has a tragic past for some of its people.
Idea 4	But together its people can have a bright future.

   Use this same structure to make an outline for your own sonnet.

Idea 1	_____
Idea 2	_____
Idea 3	_____
Idea 4	_____

Step 3.

Develop each quatrain in turn, checking the rhyme and rhythm as you go.

The following diagram shows the structure, including the relationship between the ideas, quatrains, couplet and rhyme.

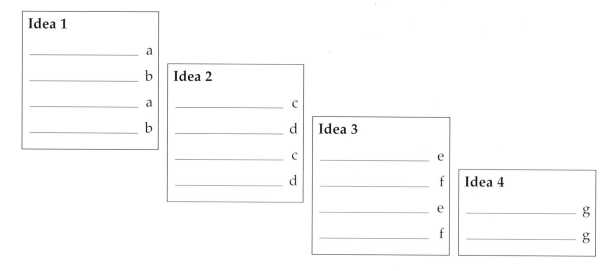

Note: You will not be able to complete your sonnet in a single draft. You may need to rewrite sections in order to get the rhythm, rhyme and ideas to work.

The sonnet as a cultural form

Like many other poets, Shakespeare wrote long sequences of sonnets in which different variations of the form were explored. Some scholars have devoted much research to finding out who the poems were written for, and have constructed complex theories about this.

Most readers don't need to know this kind of detail in order to read the sonnets, just as they don't need to know who the latest pop song is 'really' about in order to understand it. In both cases, knowledge of the form and conventions is what counts. It is this 'public' knowledge that most powerfully shapes the meanings we make from these texts.

In this way, poetry is like pop music – musicians (poets), record companies (publishers), and record buyers (readers) together form a kind of community involved in a common activity, in which certain meanings are circulated, recycled, and sometimes challenged.

Looking at form: free verse

The most common form used by modern poets is free verse. Free verse generally has no set rhyme and no strict rhythmical pattern. The lines can be of varying lengths. In this kind of poetry, it is the physical layout of the words on the page that guides the reading, so that variations in timing and smoothness can still be achieved.

On the next page are three free verse poems. Read them, and compare the form of these poems to those you have studied earlier in the chapter.

Denise Levertov is an American poet. Her poems often portray everyday scenes in simple language. 'The Frog' is an anonymously written short poem, the reading of which is guided largely by its layout on the page. The third free verse poem, Gael Turnbull's 'Thanks' is brief and tightly structured.

THE RAINWALKERS

An old man whose black face
shines golden-brown as wet pebbles
under the streetlamp, is walking
two mongrel dogs of dis-
proportionate size, in the rain,
in the relaxed early-evening avenue.

The small sleek one wants to stop,
docile to the imploring soul of the trashbasket,
but the young tall curly one
wants to walk on; the glistening sidewalk
entices him to arcane happenings.

Increasing rain. The old bareheaded man
smiles and grumbles to himself.
The lights change: the avenue's
endless nave echoes notes of
liturgical red. He drifts

between his dogs' desires.
The three of them are enveloped –
turning now to go crosstown – in their
sense of each other, of pleasure,
of weather, of corners,
of leisurely tensions between them
and private silence.

Denise Levertov

THE FROG

What a wonderful bird the frog are.

When he sit he stand almost.
When he hop he fly almost.
He ain't got no sense hardly.
He ain't got no tail hardly neither
Where he sit

Almost.

Anonymous

THANKS

Thanks, and praise for
the knot in the wood

across the grain
making the carpenter curse

where a branch sprang out
carrying sap to each leaf.

Gael Turnbull

As you can see from these examples, free verse is not completely unstructured. Free verse poets still take great care with the organisation of the text.

1. The shift to free verse has coincided with important changes in the cultural role of poetry. Some of the possible reasons for this shift are listed below. Decide which of these arguments you find most convincing, and discuss your choices with others in your class.

		Possible explanations for the rise of free verse	**Your opinion**
	a.	There is a wider range of people reading poetry now. Free verse requires less 'training' to read, and so is more accessible to a wide audience.	
	b.	There are fewer people reading poetry now, and they lack the skill to understand strict form poetry.	
	c.	The arts are more integrated into everyday life nowadays. Free verse is closer to the everyday language of people, and so seems more relevant.	
	d.	Modern printing and typesetting give the poet more control over the layout of the poem, so poets prefer to experiment with free verse rather than strict forms.	
	e.	British society in earlier times was very formal and structured, and this love of formality was reflected in the arts. Modern society is less formal, and this has made free verse forms more appealing.	
	f.	Strict forms were popular for hundreds of years, and poets explored all of their possibilities. Free verse has become popular because it is relatively new. It is a question of fashion.	
	g.	The easy availability of printed texts means that readers no longer need to memorise poems, as before. Rhyme and rhythm are therefore not needed to aid the memory.	

Can you think of other reasons why free verse has displaced some of the traditional forms?

2. There are occasions when people still use strict form poetry:

    – wedding ceremonies;
    – obituaries (death notices);
    – some greeting cards.

Can you add to this list? Why might people use strict form poetry in these cases?

Looking back at form

In this section you have studied a number of poetic forms and discussed their different functions. Write a report in which you summarise what you have learned. Make notes about the following points.

1. Your definition of 'poetic form'.
2. The influence of form on the reading and writing of poetry.
3. The relationship between culture and poetic form.

Share your report with others in your class.

FAMOUS 'FIRST DRAFTS'

Poets very rarely succeed in writing a poem in one go. Most have to re-draft their poems many times before they achieve the combination of words, sounds, images and ideas that will produce the results they want. Often the poems undergo significant changes in this process. A lot can be learned about the conventions of poetry by studying these drafts.

This section brings together the work you have done on words, form and meaning, through the study of two famous poems. In the work that follows you will see how the poems were shaped and drafted by their writers, and you will discuss the way conventions of description, comparison and form have contributed to this shaping.

The Tyger

'The Tyger' is by William Blake, an English poet and artist. It was written around 1793 as part of a collection of poems exploring ideas of innocence and corruption in the world. The poem presents the tiger as an awe-inspiring animal, both beautiful and disturbing.

The poem is structured as a series of questions, which can be summarised like this:

> What kind of creator could produce such a fearful creature?
> How could an animal like this have come about?
> What does the existence of such an animal say about the world we live in?

Read through the poem at least twice before reading on.

THE TYGER

Tyger! Tyger! burning bright
In the forests of the night
What immortal hand or eye
Could frame thy fearful symmetry?

In what distant deeps or skies
Burnt the fire of thine eyes?
On what wings dare he aspire?
What the hand dare seize the fire?

And what shoulder, & what art,
Could twist the sinews of thy heart?
And when thy heart began to beat,
What dread hand & what dread feet?

What the hammer? what the chain?
In what furnace was thy brain?
What the anvil? what dread grasp
Dare its deadly terrors clasp?

When the stars threw down their spears,
And water'd heaven with their tears,
Did he smile his work to see?
Did he who made the Lamb make thee?

Tyger! Tyger! burning bright
In the forests of the night,
What immortal hand or eye
Dare frame they fearful symmetry?

William Blake

Exploring the poem

The poem suggests that the tiger's fearsome qualities have been gathered from all over the world, and assembled by a mysterious and awesome creator. This idea can be seen in stanza two, as the following paraphrase shows.

Stanza two	Paraphrase
In what distant deeps or skies Burnt the fire of thine eyes? On what wings dare he aspire? What the hand dare seize the fire?	Where did the fire in your eyes come from? From what oceans or skies was it taken? Who was it that flew to these places to collect the fire? What hand seized it and brought it back?

The paraphrase shows that the language of the poem is often very compressed. For example, in this stanza the line, 'What the hand dare seize the fire?' could be read as 'What/whose was the hand that dared to seize this fire?'

Because of this compression, the poem requires careful reading.

Activities

1. Work in a pair or a small group, to create your own paraphrase of *one* other stanza in the poem. By allocating a different stanza to each group, the class can work on the whole poem. (You will need to consider the surrounding stanzas also, when writing your paraphrase.)

2. When the paraphrases have been written, invite each pair or group to present its paraphrase to the class and explain the meaning of their stanza.

3. After hearing the paraphrases, read the poem again.

Discussion

In Blake's society, it was thought by many that all things were created for a purpose, and that the world reflected the qualities of its creator. 'The Tyger' can be read with this belief in mind.

1. What does the poem seem to imply about the world and its creator? The following statements might give you some starting points for discussion. Make a note of those you think are supported by the poem.

   a. The world is beautiful.
   b. The world is dangerous.
   c. The creator is powerful.
   d. The creator is threatening.
   e. The world exists for the benefit of humans.
   f. Humans are merely part of creation.
   g. Humans are irrelevant in the world.
   h. Appearances reveal the truth of things.

   Are there statements you could add to the list? If so, write them down.

2. Use these statements to discuss your reading of the poem with others in your group or class.

3. What image of the creator is developed in the poem?

Writing

Before going on, write a brief (one paragraph) report on the poem. In your report say what the poem is about, what ideas or themes you think it develops, and how the content and themes are conveyed. This should be a summing up of your ideas about the poem.

Shaping the poem

Like all poems, 'The Tyger' has been shaped by the associations and expectations that are shared by some readers and writers.

In writing his poem, Blake had to take account of the conventions of language and form that applied to poetry in eighteenth century England. Some of this shaping can be seen in the early drafts of the poem. What follows is an earlier version of 'The Tyger', showing the first draft and a number of additions that Blake made before the final version.

Read through the draft, and compare it to the final version on page 89.

Draft of 'The Tyger'

Tyger Tyger burning bright
In the forests of the night
What immortal hand or eye
~~Could~~ frame thy fearful symmetry
~~Dare~~

Burnt in
~~In what~~ distant deeps or skies
~~The cruel~~
~~Burnt the~~ fire of thine eyes
On what wings dare he aspire
What the hand dare seize the fire

Burnt in distant deeps or skies
The cruel fire of thine eyes
Could heart descend or wings aspire

What the hand dare seize the fire
dare he ~~smile~~ laugh
And ~~did he laugh~~ his work to see

And what shoulder & what art
Could twist the sinews of thy heart
And when thy heart began to beat
What dread hand & what dread feet

ankle
~~What the shoulder what the knee~~
Dare
~~Did~~ he who made the lamb make thee
When the stars threw down their spears

~~Could fetch it from the furnace deep~~
~~And in they horrid ribs dare steep~~
~~In the well of sanguine woe~~
~~In what clay & in what mould~~
~~Were thy eyes of fury roll'd~~

Where   where
~~What~~ the hammer ~~what~~ the chain
In what furnace was thy brain

dread grasp
What the anvil what ~~arm arm grasp clasp~~
~~Could~~ its deadly terrors ~~clasp grasp~~ clasp
Dare

And water'd heaven with their tears
Tyger tyger burning bright
In the forests of the night
What immortal hand & eye
Dare ~~form~~ they fearful symmetry
          frame

Language

The wording of 'The Tyger' has gone through a number of changes from draft to final copy. The changes seem to have been guided by a number of factors:

- the effect of sound;
- the effect of likely associations;
- the development of an idea;
- the development of a pattern to the poem.

These are conventions of form and language that guide the reading and writing of poetry.

Activities

1. Listed below are two changes of wording that the poet has experimented with. For each example, select the reason in the right hand column that you think best explains the change, or write your own reason.

Draft	Final	Possible reasons for change
Did he laugh his work to see?	Did he smile his work to see?	'smile' is more ambiguous about the creator's purpose 'smile' implies satisfaction, not amusement 'laugh' breaks the sombre mood of the poem 'smile' makes the creator seem friendly
What the ankle what the knee	And what shoulder, & what art?	'shoulder' creates an image of powerful activity 'ankle and knee' are unintentionally funny 'art' presents the creator as more than just a 'builder' the first version is too repetitive

2. Find *three* other changes of wording, and give your own explanations for the changes that were made. Share your findings.

3. The following lines and image were rejected for the final version of the poem:

   'In what clay and in what mould
   Were thy eyes of fury roll'd'

   Can you suggest why this image was not used?

4. Find another image that was rejected, and discuss the possible reasons for it being left out.

Form

A number of patterns, such as rhyme and rhythm, contribute to the *form* of Blake's poem.

Activities

1. Work with a partner to list all of the formal features such as rhyme and rhythm that you can find in the poem.

2. Look for places where Blake's choice of form has helped shape the words and images of the poem (for example, places where words have been left out to make the rhythm work).

Writing

Write your own poem using Blake's text as a model. You can keep the structure of 'The Tyger' but change the subject matter and tone (or the manner – serious or humorous – that you use.)

You could try to make your own statement about nature and creation through your choice of animal, the tone, and the images you use. You could write about an animal that you find awe-inspiring, or create a humorous parody. Here are two examples to help you get started.

THE HAMSTER

Hamster! Hamster! snoring soft
After all the food you've scoffed
What misguided eye, what hand
Could make your features quite so bland?

THE WHALE

Whale! Whale! floating free
In the silence of the sea
What great forces, what slow time
Gave birth to thy form sublime?

Anthem For Doomed Youth

The next poem was written by Wilfred Owen, a British poet and soldier who wrote about his experiences in the First World War. Most of his poems were written in the period 1915-1918. 'Anthem for Doomed Youth' can be read as a comment on the tragic waste of young men's lives in wartime. Before reading the poem, consider these questions and write down your predictions.

1. What would you expect to find in a poem which is titled as an 'Anthem'?
2. What are some of the possible attitudes that could be expressed in such a poem? (Patriotism? Glorification? Despair? Pride? Others?)
3. What are your expectations about the language of a poem about war?
4. What kind of form would you expect in a poem on this subject?

Read the poem a number of times, then work through the activities that follow.

ANTHEM FOR DOOMED YOUTH

What passing bells for these who die as cattle?
   Only the monstrous anger of the guns.
   Only the stuttering rifles' rapid rattle
Can patter out their hasty orisons.   (orison= a prayer)
No mockeries now for them, no prayers nor bells,
   Nor any voice of mourning save the choirs, –
The shrill demented choirs of wailing shells,
   And bugles calling for them from sad shires.   (shire = county or district)

What candles may be held to speed them all?
   Not in the hands of boys, but in their eyes
Shall shine the holy glimmers of goodbyes.
   The pallor of girls' brows shall be their pall;   (pallor = paleness)
Their flowers the tenderness of patient minds,
And each slow dusk a drawing down of blinds.

Wilfred Owen

THE POETRY LIBRARY

Exploring the poem

Owen's poem can be read as a series of comparisons that show the difference between death on the battlefield in wartime and death 'at home' in peacetime. Here are two such comparisons from the first four lines of the poem.

Peacetime	Wartime
People die 'naturally'.	People are slaughtered like cattle.
Bells are rung in villages to call the mourners.	Death is accompanied by the sounds of gunfire.

Re-read the first four lines of the poem with these contrasts in mind.

Activities

1. Listed below are some other customs that the poem associates with death in peacetime. Fill in the wartime equivalent by referring back to the poem.

Peacetime	Wartime
People say quiet prayers for the dead.	Only the 'stuttering rifles' 'speak', with a 'rapid rattle'.
Church choirs sing hymns for the dead.	
Altar boys hold candles to light the soul's way to heaven.	
A white shroud is draped over the coffin.	
Mourners place flowers on the grave.	
The blinds are drawn in the dead person's home after the funeral to mark their passing.	

Compare your answers with others in your class or group.

2. Like many poems, Owen's text can be read as a contribution to a culture's ongoing 'discussion' about some topic – in this case, war and death. Below are some of the things it might be saying about this topic. Choose those statements you think the poem supports.

   a. Death on the battlefield has its own kind of dignity.
   b. Death on the battlefield is tragic and undignified.
   c. Death on the battlefield is both tragic and glorious.
   d. Death should be marked by rituals.
   e. Life and death are governed by fate.
   f. War has a life of its own, and young men are its victims.
   g. War teaches boys to be men.

Use these statements as starting points for your discussion of the poem.

Language and form

Owen's poem is notable for its use of words that trigger strong and complex associations. Many of these words have religious connotations. 'Anthem for Doomed Youth' is a sonnet. From your work on sonnets, (pages 80–86), you know that sonnets not only have a strict formal structure, but also common functions or purposes.

Activity

1. Work with a partner to investigate both of these aspects of the poem, and say how they help shape the ideas generated by the text. You should consider the following points.

    1. The wording of the title, especially the words 'anthem' and 'doomed'.
    2. The use of personification (representing objects as if they were alive) in these phrases:

        – the 'monstrous anger of the guns' (line 2);
        – the 'stuttered' prayers of the rifles (lines 3–4);
        – the mourning of 'shrill demented choirs' (line 7);
        – the 'calling' of bugles (line 8).

    3. How the sonnet form contributes to the effect of the poem.

2. Write a brief (one paragraph) report on the poem. In your report say what the poem is about, what ideas or themes you think it develops, and how the content and themes are conveyed. This should be a summing up of your ideas about the poem.

Shaping the poem

Following are three earlier drafts of 'Anthem for Doomed Youth'. The changes in these drafts affect many aspects of the poem, including: language, form, ideas and associations.

Read through the various drafts, then work through the activities that follow.

Draft 1

passing
What ~~minute~~ bells for these who die so fast?
~~solemn~~
– Only the monstrous anger of our guns.
Let the majestic insults of their iron mouths
requiem
Be as the ~~priest words~~ of their burials.
Of choristers and holy music, none;
Nor any voice of mourning save the wail
The long drawn wail of high far-sailing shells.

to light
What candles may we hold ~~for~~ these lost? ~~souls?~~
Not in the hands of boys, but in their eyes
shine the ~~tapers~~   the holy ~~tapers~~ candles
Shall / many ~~candles shine; and I will light them~~
~~holy~~ flames: to

Women's wide-spreaded arms shall be their wreaths,
And pallor of girl's cheeks shall be their palls
mortal
Their flowers, the tenderness of all men's minds,
~~comrades~~
each slow   rough men's
And ~~every~~ Dusk a drawing-down of blinds.

Draft 2

> ### for
> ### Anthem ~~to~~ Dead Youth
>
> What passing bells for you who die in herds?
>   the
> – Only the monstrous anger of ~~more~~ guns.
> – Only the stuttering rifles' rattled words
> Can patter out your hasty orisons.
>   choirs
> No chants for you, nor blams, nor wreaths, nor bells
>   shells
>   Nor any voice of mourning, save the choirs,
> And long-drawn sighs
> ~~The shrill demented choirs~~ of wailing shells;
>   And bugles calling for you from sad shires.
>
> What candles may be held to speed you all?
>   Not in the hands of boys, but in their eyes
> Shall   ~~and gleams~~ our
> ~~Shall~~ shine ~~the~~ holy lights / of ~~long~~ goodbyes
>   must
> The pallor of girls' brows ~~shall~~ be your pall;
>
>   ~~broken simple frail~~
> Your flowers, the tenderness of ~~mortal~~ minds
>   ~~pain white~~
>   ~~grief innocent~~
>   comrades'
> And each slow dusk, a drawing-down of blinds.

Draft 3

> ### Doomed
> ### Anthem for ~~Dead~~ Youth
>
> What passing bells for these dumb-dying cattle?
> – Only the monstrous anger of more guns!
> Only the stuttering rifles' rapid rattle
> Can patter out their hasty orisons.
>
> No chants for them, nor wreaths, nor asphodels
>   Nor any voice of mourning save the choirs,
> The shrill demented choirs of wailing shells;
>   And bugles calling for them from sad shires.
>
> What candles may be held to speed them all?
>   Not in the hands of boys, but in their eyes
> Shall shine the holy gleams of their goodbyes.
>   The pallor of girls' brows shall be their pall.
>
> Their flowers the tenderness of silent minds,
> And each slow dusk a drawing down of blinds.

Activities

1. Work through the drafts with a partner to find examples of the following changes. Write down your examples under the following headings.

    1. A change that improves the sound of the poem.

    2. A phrase that has been compressed into a word.

    3. A change that improves the associations of a word or phrase.

    4. A shift in the ideas of the poem.

    5. A change that strengthens the form of the poem (eg, by improving the rhyme, rhythm, balance or pattern of the text).

2. Write briefly about the effects of each of these changes.

3. Share your findings with others in a small group or class discussion.

Going further

4. Prepare a reading of the poem with a partner or with your group. Experiment with ways of reading the poem that will convey your ideas about its mood and meanings.

5. Compare Wilfred Owen's 'Anthem for Doomed Youth' with Rupert Brooke's 'The Soldier' on page 19. What similarities and differences can you find on the following points:

    – ideas about war?

    – the language of the poems?

    – the forms used?

    – the assumptions implied by each poem?

6. Present your findings in an essay, comparing and contrasting the treatment of war and death in these two poems.

    You could look back to pages 47–51 to remind yourself of one approach to writing a comparison of two poems.

The Python guide to poetry

In one of their early comic books, the Monty Python Team (a troupe of British comedy writers and actors) presented a selection of famous poems in 'first-draft' form. Two examples follow.

John Keats   *Ode to a Nightingale*

Finished poem:

> My heart aches, and a drowsy numbness pains
> My sense, as though of hemlock I had drunk,
> Or emptied some dull opiate to the drains
> One minute past, and Lethe-wards had sunk ...

The Pythons' first draft:

>   aches
> My heart ~~goes ping pong~~
>
>   drowsy
> And a ~~lousy~~ numbness pains my sense
>
>   Hemlock
> As though of ~~Watneys~~ I had drunk,
>
>   emptied some dull opiate to the drains
> Or ~~thrown up all over your carpet~~
>
> ~~All right officer, I'll come quietly~~ ...

T.S. Eliot   *The Love Song of J. Alfred Prufrock*

Finished poem:

> Let us go, then, you and I
> When the evening is spread out against the sky
> Like a patient etherised upon a table;
> Let us go, through certain half deserted streets,
> The muttering retreats
> Of restless nights in one-night cheap hotels ...

The Pythons' first draft:

> Let us go, then, you and I
> ~~K K K Katy, B B Beautiful Katy~~
>
> When the evening is spread out against the sky
> ~~You're the only girl that I adore~~
>
> Like a patient etherised upon a table;
> ~~When the m-moon shines, over the cowshed~~
>
> Let us go, through certain half deserted streets,
> ~~I'll be waiting at the k k k kitchen door.~~

Activity

Create your own 'famous first drafts', based on poems you have studied. These could make an entertaining display in your classroom.

5.

Writing a Poetry Critique

I'D LIKE –

I'd like to know

what this whole show

is all about

before it's out.

Piet Hein

WHY WRITE A CRITIQUE?

Like movies, novels, and music, poems are texts that people use to reflect on their lives and experiences. Poems can have an impact on people's thinking not only through the things they might say to their readers, but through the discussions that readers have *with each other* about poems. This kind of discussion about texts is one of the ways that members of a community share their ideas and shape their values.

If you have read movie, video and music reviews in magazines, you already have some idea of why people write critiques. Poetry critiques are like reviews: they give the reader some information about the text, and they provoke discussion among readers about the ideas and issues raised by the poem. They also give the writer's opinion or judgment about whether a text is worth reading ('critique' comes from the Greek word *kritikos*, which means 'a judge').

Often readers will disagree with a review, but even by disagreeing they may be led to sharpen their own ideas about the text. Some magazines publish letters from readers who want to have their own say about a text. Writing a critique is a bit like contributing to a public discussion about a text and the issues it raises.

This means that an effective critique must do more than just list the techniques used in a poem. *It must have something to say about the poem* – an opinion about its artistic effectiveness and the ideas it addresses. It should say something that will make others want to read it.

Seasons

On pages 101 and 102 are two responses, written by high school students, to a short poem called 'Seasons'. Before looking at the essays, read the poem yourself a number of times.

SEASONS

Spring like a timid child
courts you with a giggle.
Lazy summer days like whores
drape themselves on deckchairs.
Autumn's slow wrinkles
smile and crease deeper
as you rise to say hello.
Winter taps her frigid limbs
on the brittle silvered panes.

Jessica Cameron

Discussion

Before going on, discuss the poem briefly in your groups. You might consider the following points in your discussion.

The idea. (What is the idea in the poem? Is it clever?)
The way this idea is developed. (How effective is it?)
Your personal reaction. (What is your reading of the poem?)

Two critiques

The short critiques that follow show the difference between a response that has something to say about the poem, and one that merely recites a list of terms. Most teachers of literature would give high marks to one of the following critiques, and low marks to the other.

Read the critiques, then work through the activities that follow.

Critique 1.

The Same Old "Seasons"

"Seasons" is basically a descriptive poem. It represents the seasons as if they were living people, and it gives a fresh way of thinking about an everyday aspect of the world. However, it also ends up by reinforcing certain stereotypes, and for that reason I find it unpleasant even though it is quite clever.

The poem begins with a description of spring as a "timid child" that is playful. Through this comparison the poem attaches an emotion and a set of associations to the concept of spring. The reader finds the image of the timid child charming, and this feeling becomes associated with spring. As it develops, the poem uses the same technique to attach feelings to the other seasons.

The order in which the seasons are presented is important for the effectiveness of the poem – spring, summer, autumn, winter. These seasons are often used in poetry to represent the stages in a person's life, from young to old. In this poem, this idea is used in reverse. Different human qualities are being used to say something about the seasons. These qualities include giggling (for spring), laziness (for summer), wrinkles (for autumn) and "frigid limbs" (for winter). In this way, human life becomes reflected in the seasons of nature.

The problem with this poem, however, is the way it uses images of women in its descriptions. The description of summer as a "lazy whore" I think is offensive, because it uses the stereotype of a prostitute as a lazy and self-centred woman. The "whores" are described as draped "on deckchairs" (l. 4). The way this image is placed in the sequence also implies that whores are young (and maybe beautiful), something which is not necessarily true. The other images are also stereotyped as a giggling young girl, a wrinkled middle-aged woman and a cold "frigid" old woman. These are ideas about women that people have been trying to shake off for years. In this poem, the ideas are made to seem natural by matching them with the seasons of nature.

The poem might have been more effective if it tried to break down the stereotypes, for example by describing spring as a grandmother's giggle, or autumn as a young girl in bare feet. This would really have given the reader something to think about. Instead, the poem has been put together from very typical ideas about women.

The poem is quite good in its techniques. It makes good use of comparisons, and many of its images are effective in portraying the seasons. But, because it reinforces stereotyped views of women, I personally find this poem unpleasant.

Greg Allan

Critique 2

Essay on "Seasons"

The poem "Seasons" by Jessica Cameron is mainly a description of the seasons, which are compared to a human at different ages of life. The seasons begin with spring, and the person's life begins as a young child. The other seasons of summer, autumn and winter are described as a young whore, a wrinkled woman (perhaps in her middle years) and an old woman with cold stiff limbs.

The main technique in this poem is imagery and personification. Imagery is where the poem creates a vivid picture for the reader. This is done in the poem by describing a feature of the woman at different ages, such as the sexy whore, the slow, wrinkled woman, and the old lady with frigid limbs tapping on the window pane. The images give the reader an impression of what the seasons are like.

The writer is also using personification. This is when a thing that is not alive is being described as if it were a human being. By personification the poet makes it seem as if the seasons have personalities, like people.

The poem is written in free verse form. The structure of the poem is as a single verse of nine lines. There is no rhythm or rhyme pattern. Each of the seasons is described in a two line image, except for autumn, which has three lines.

This is an effective poem because it uses images and personification to describe the subject matter, which is the seasons.

John Ramsay

Discussion

Which of these critiques is more likely to provoke discussion about the poem? Do you agree with what this student has to say?

Thinking through the critiques

Most teachers would agree that the first critique is the more successful. This writer offers a clear opinion about the poem, as well as providing an explanation of how the poem works. By contrast, the writer of the second essay seems to be working through a checklist of terms and techniques (image, personification, rhythm, rhyme) without really forming a view of the poem as a whole.

Activities

1. The first paragraph of Greg Allen's critique on page 101 contains a sentence that sums up his reading of the poem. <u>Underline</u> the sentence.

2. Which of the following best explains Greg Allen's objection to the poem?

   The poem is not effective in its use of comparison.
   The poem contains values and attitudes that are undesirable.
   The poem is not original enough.
   The poem offers a misleading view of nature.

3. Based on your reading of his essay, which of the following beliefs about poetry do you think Greg Allen supports? (You may choose more than one.)

    a. Poetry is irrelevant to modern life.
    b. Poetry can shape a society's values.
    c. Poetry should aim to improve the world.
    d. The most important aspect of poetry is ideas.
    e. The most important aspect of poetry is technique.
    f. Poetry should strive to be original.
    g. Poetry should strive to be responsible.

Do you agree with these views?

4. The essay by John Ramsay suggests a different attitude to poetry. What beliefs or ideas are implied by his essay?

5. There are other differences between these critiques. Discuss these differences, and say how they affect the success of each essay.

Model critiques

In this section you will read a range of critiques in response to a more complex poem. You will also read comments from teachers, about each critique. This will help you develop your ideas about what is required from a good poetry critique.

The 'critics' in this section are responding to a poem by Gerard Manly Hopkins. Hopkins was a British poet and also a priest. The poem was written in 1880. In this poem, the speaker is apparently talking to a young child who has been saddened by the falling of autumn leaves.

To familiarise yourself with the poem, read it through a number of times, then do the activities that follow.

SPRING AND FALL
(To a Young Child)

1   Margaret, are you grieving
      Over Goldengrove unleaving?
      Leaves, like the things of man, you
      With your fresh thoughts care for, can you?
5   Ah! As the heart grows older
      It will come to such sights colder
      By and by, nor spare a sigh
      Though worlds of wanwood leafmeal lie;   (wanwood = pale woodland)
      And yet you will weep and know why.
10   Now, no matter child the name:
      Sorrows springs are the same.
      Nor mouth had, no nor mind, expressed
      What heart heard of, ghost guessed:
      It is the blight man was born for,
15   It is Margaret you mourn for.

Gerard Manly Hopkins

1. Hopkins' poem is complex in its ideas and language. Below is a simplified paraphrase that will help you to make sense of the text. Each two-line paraphrase relates to a section of the poem, but the order has been jumbled.

   Working with a partner, put the paraphrase sections into the correct order by numbering them from 1 to 8. Say which lines of the poem the paraphrase refers to.

   The first section has been numbered for you.

	Paraphrase of 'Spring and Fall'	Lines
	When you grow up, you won't be upset by such things.	
	Whatever we call it, all sadness comes from the same source.	
	You will still be sad, but you will understand why you are sad.	
	Are you so young that falling leaves sadden you more than human life?	
	Even if whole forests of pale trees lie rotting on the earth.	
1	Margaret, are you sad about the falling leaves in the grove?	1-2
	It is the idea of death that disturbs you, and your own mortality that saddens you.	
	We cannot say why we are sad, but we know inside ourselves what the cause is.	

2. Readers may find a number of themes in this poem. Which of the following themes do you think are most strongly developed?

   The beauty of nature.
   The sadness of growing up.
   The sadness of human mortality.
   The wisdom of old age.
   The innocence of childhood.

   Discuss your choice with others in your group or class.

3. Write a one-paragraph report on the poem, describing what it is about, and what themes you think are explored through the poem.

Readings of the poem

The essays you are about to read were written by students in response to the following question.

> Outline the main ideas in Hopkins' poem, and show how these ideas are developed. Give your opinion of the poem's effectiveness.

This question asks readers to perform three tasks: outline the ideas, show the method of development, and make a judgment about its success. The critiques that follow all explore the poem from different perspectives, but each one attempts to do these three tasks. (The students' names have been changed.)

Critique 1

The Theme of Death in "Spring and Fall"

In the poem "Spring and Fall" by Gerard Manly Hopkins, a young child has become sad about the falling leaves in her favourite grove of trees. This event is used to develop the main idea in the poem, which is the theme of aging and death, and how this fact of life is the source of all sadness for human beings.

The poem's idea is developed as a dramatic monologue. The reader 'overhears' one side of a conversation, the things that are said (or perhaps only thought) by an adult who has seen Margaret's reaction to the falling leaves. It is also structured with a question and answer design. It begins with the adult asking why Margaret is sad: "Margaret are you grieving / over Goldengrove unleaving?" (l. 1–2). The second question is harder to follow, but seems to say, Are you still so young that falling leaves upset you, instead of "the things of man"? This means that Margaret is still upset by things of nature, but the adult knows she will learn to be more sad about things that affect mankind.

The rest of the poem is an answer to these first questions. The adult says that as Margaret grows older, she will be less worried by the falling leaves. She will still be sad, but at least she will know why: "And yet you will weep and know why" (l. 9). This point is emphasised by the structure of the poem, which makes this line stand out. The poem is written in rhyming pairs, but this line is extra; it adds a third rhyme (sigh/lie/why) and seems to be a pause or turnaround in the poem, where it finally begins to explain the real cause of Margaret's sad feelings.

The adult says that Margaret is sad because she has just learned that nothing lasts forever. Her feelings are more advanced than her intelligence, and she is sad because she knows deep down that her own life won't last forever either, just like the leaves. This is shown in the lines: "What heart heard of, ghost guessed:/ It is the blight man was born for,/ It is Margaret you mourn for" (l. 13–15). This seems to mean that fear of old age and death is the reason why we feel sad about other changes and events. The line "sorrow's springs are the same" (l. 11) basically says all sadness is the same. This means that Margaret is sad for herself, even though she doesn't know it. Personally, I don't agree with this idea. Hopkins seems to think that human beings are the most important thing on earth, and that we cannot be sad about anything else. This seems a rather old-fashioned idea, though it was probably believed when the poem was written.

For modern readers this poem may not be very effective. The language in the poem is old-fashioned and quite difficult, with unusual or made up words such as "wanwood" and "leafmeal" (l. 8), and some sections where the wording is difficult to follow (lines 3–4, for example). It is also very artificial, as people don't really speak or think in this way. Modern readers prefer more realistic speech in poems. All this means that many readers would not bother with the poem. However, for readers in the past it would be a good poem, I think, because the ideas are interesting once you have taken the trouble to work out what is being said. For readers who appreciate poetic language, the poem would be effective in triggering images and feelings. "Worlds of wanwood" suggests vast fields of pale woodlands, and "leafmeal" suggests layers of decaying leaves. The repetition of "w" and "l" sounds in this line also creates a sense of softness that is good for portraying the gentle fall of leaves. These examples show the poet is skilled at manipulating the reader's emotions and thoughts.

In spite of its old fashionedness, the poem presents the ideas of age and death in a very different way, by combining an interesting question and answer structure with good use of sounds and word meanings. In this way it still can be relevant to readers today as an example of interesting poetry from the past.

'Tan'

Critique 2

"Spring and Fall"

I don't think this is a very effective poem. It uses rather wussy language and I don't think anyone would read it unless they were studying it in a poetry class. It is basically about a young girl who is sad because the leaves are falling at a place called Goldengrove (probably a park or forest). I think the poet's idea is that only young children are so sensitive, and soon they lose this emotional dimension in their lives and become much harder, as it says her heart will become "colder". The main idea is about how people become insensitive as they grow older.

The poem is a dramatic monologue, with a speaker who is older than the young girl, maybe a parent or an uncle. We find out the poem's meaning by listening to the speaker as he talks to the young girl. Her speech is not reported, but we can work out how she is feeling and acting from what the speaker is saying. For example, we can tell from the opening lines that Margaret has been crying over the leaves, and that she wants to know why such sad things happen.

Giving readers only one side of the conversation is quite effective because it makes the reader respond in a certain way. Because we can only hear what the parent or whoever is saying, we tend to side with that person and accept their view of things. That way the poet can make us listen to his ideas, without making it too obvious. It is like overhearing a conversation, and so you listen harder to find out what is going on. Also, it would have been hard to make the poem work as a dialogue, with both characters talking, because the poem has a very high tone (very formal). To make a young person's speech fit in with this would change the tone or else sound very false, because young people would not talk like this.

The development of the ideas is through what the speaker says to Margaret. The argument has a number of stages. First, it asks Margaret why she is sad. Then it says that as she grows older, she won't worry about little things like falling leaves, even if the whole world was covered with leaves. This is conveyed in the lines, "though worlds of wanwood leafmeal lie / and yet you will weep and know why" (l. 8–9). This means that even though she will become more hard hearted, she will still weep, and she will know why she is weeping. It will be because she is grieving the lost feelings that she doesn't have any more. The poet says that this is what makes all people sad, the fact that life makes them harder and not so likely to cry over little things.

I don't think this is a very believable view. I think people can still be sad when they get older. People can still cry at movies and such, and lots of old people can be very sentimental, especially about young children. In a way, this poem is contradicting its own idea because it is actually a sentimental view of a young child as being innocent. So in some ways it could be seen as not being effective.

'Faysal'

Critique 3

"Spring and Fall"

The main idea of Gerard's poem is that a young child (Margaret) is grieving over something that has happened, and the poet comforts her by saying that things are not so bad. She should enjoy life while she is young because soon she will be older and really will know true sadness. It is an effective poem because it is well constructed.

Critique 3 continued:

The poem is carefully designed. It uses rhyming pairs of lines to create the form of an aa bb cc ddd ee ff gg rhyming pattern, with one line extra in the "d" section. This is a strict form. It also has a strong rhythm in many of the lines. This shows that the poem was written at a time when people enjoyed very structured writing and may have enjoyed reciting poetry. Now there is much more free verse, as people can read poems in books and do not need to memorise them.

The ideas of the poem are developed with great care. It shows how the young child is more emotional and is affected by things like a grove of trees with its leaves falling off. But the parent is older and is not. The parent's heart is older and "colder" (l. 6). This is because the parent knows that things in nature like groves of leaves can lie and give a false sense of sadness, as in the lines: "worlds of wanwood leafmeal lie" (l. 8). This means that the world can give misleading feelings to the inexperienced person.

The poem contains many associations that are triggered by the words. Some of these are "fresh thoughts," "leafmeal," "sorrows springs" and "ghost guessed". These are words that give the reader an emotional reaction, to shape how the reader feels. There is also a good use of sound in the poem, such as "spare a sigh," "worlds of wanwood," and "leafmeal lie," where sounds are repeated for their effect (alliteration).

Overall, I think this is a successful poem because of its use of these techniques. Although it is difficult to read at first, it has an interesting idea. It shows how children are saddened by passing phases, but the older people are saddened by life.

'Veronika'

Critique 4

"Spring and Fall" - A Female View

"Spring and Fall" is a very patriarchal poem. It puts forward a view of life that says old people are wiser than the young, and that they can be trusted to give guidance and truth to the next generation. The poet, Gerard Manly Hopkins, was also a religious minister, which was a very male dominated profession in the 1800s, and his view of the world can be seen in the poem.

In the poem a young girl has been crying because autumn has come and the leaves are falling in Goldengrove. She is made out as a sensitive young girl who gets upset at small things (this is a stereotype of women generally). The person speaking in the poem is older, and seems to be a father figure. This person comments on the young girl, or perhaps is giving advice to her in the form of an interior monologue, where we hear the thoughts going on in his mind. The father figure explains that in the future the young girl will have more important things to grieve over other than the falling leaves. The poem says she will "come to such sights colder / By and by nor spare a sigh" (l. 6), even if the whole world is full of bare forests and rotting leaves (l. 8)

The idea developed in the poem is that the sadness of childhood is like a premonition of things to come. The speaker says that Margaret thinks she is sad because of the leaves, but really she is sad because she has learned a fact of life, that things grow old and decay. It says that this is what makes us sad, the fact that we will all age and die. Margaret is too young to understand that the seasons have a cycle and that the leaves will come back again in the spring, so to her the autumn "fall" looks like an image of death. This explains the sub-title of the poem, which says that this is what spring and autumn must seem like "to a young child". (It also means that the lines are being spoken to a young child, so the title has two meanings.)

Critique 4 continued:

The writer has used language to manipulate how the reader will react to the poem. It is full of soft sounds, like the fall of leaves, for example, "fresh," and has a gentle rhythm, such as "by and by, nor spare a sigh" (l. 7). This suits a poem that is philosophical and not full of action. It also contains good descriptions such as "fresh thoughts," which gives the idea of a new mind that is still "green," and also the word "leafmeal," which gives the idea of soft mouldy leaves decaying. The rhyme helps give the poem a structure and makes it seem more old fashioned and formal, so that it suits the idea of a father figure giving wisdom to the young.

I find this a very male-oriented poem, not that males would be the only ones to read it, but because it has such a strong father-figure in it. It builds up the idea of a father as head of the family, or even as head of the church. A lot of older poetry had religious themes, and this one is a bit like a minister speaking to the young children and explaining God's plan to them. A common religious idea was original sin, which said that people were doomed to lead sad lives because of what Adam and Eve had done in the garden of Eden. In this poem, it says that sadness is "the blight man was born for" (l. 14), as if Margaret has this original sin also. The fact that Hopkins was a priest means that he would have believed in this idea.

In modern society people are more questioning about the truth and who is wise. Therefore I don't think this poem will appeal so much to the modern reader. Women especially are against the father figure idea. In a modern poem it might be more likely to have a mother and her child, and I think the mother would be more understanding. Her message to the child might be more comforting and optimistic, instead of saying "it's a sad world and you're stuck with it." This is a skilful poem in its techniques, but I don't accept its message.

'Kim'

Activity

1. Re-read the four critiques and rank them in order from best to worst. In working out your rankings, you should consider the following points.

    a. Whether the essay has 'something to say'.
    b. Whether the essay deals with the question successfully.
    c. The quality of the analysis, or 'reading,' of the poem.
    d. The quality of the writing.

2. Record your rankings by placing the numbers 1 to 4 in the first column below.

Essay	Your ranking	Group ranking	Reasons
1. Tan			
2. Faysal			
3. Veronika			
4. Kim			

3. When you have recorded your ranking, discuss the essays in a small group. Through discussion, try to arrive at an agreed ranking for the four pieces, and record this in the 'group' column. Make notes on the reason for your decisions.

Teacher responses

The four essays on pages 105–108 were shown to a range of teachers, who commented on the strengths and weaknesses of each one. Printed below is a selection of their responses.

Read the following comments and compare them with your own observations. (Only the teachers' initials have been given.)

1. Tan

This is a good essay. There's evidence that the student understands the ideas, and the essay is well structured. The essay explains very well how the form of the poem (dramatic monologue, question-answer) is used to develop the ideas about youth and age, and death. The reading of line 9 as a turning point is good (it should be noted that this line is also the end of a sentence, which adds to the strength of the pause). The discussion of language could be developed further. It seems to have been added as an afterthought and doesn't really fit into the main discussion. The rules for quotation have been followed accurately. It's quite a polished effort. (S.N.)

2. Faysal

This essay starts badly. A comment like "wussy" language is not appropriate. However, the student does offer quite a good reading of the poem. His reading of the theme as a loss of sensitivity is unusual, but quite well argued I think. He makes good observations about the use of dramatic monologue and how it can shape the reader's response. I think more could have been said about the sentimental aspects of the poem – it's an interesting point, and it shouldn't have been made only in the final paragraph. Some of the expression should be more formal – phrases such as "wussy language" and "basically about" sound too much like casual speech rather than polished writing. There should also be more discussion of the language in the poem. It isn't as bad as I thought at first, but needs polishing. (A.N.)

3. Veronika

This essay doesn't really explain what the idea of the poem is, what the "true sadness" is that humans suffer from. This suggests to me that the student isn't sure. The essay spends a lot of time talking about features of the poem, such as the rhyme pattern, without saying why these things are important. Paragraphs are not well developed: for example, par. three begins with a comment about <u>how</u> the ideas are developed, but the rest of the paragraph talks about other things, other ideas. The word "lie" in line 8 has been misread, and the essay doesn't justify this reading. Par. four lists emotive words, but doesn't say what the emotions or connotations are – it's just a list. There's also some confusion between the speaker in the poem and the actual poet (this happens in the first paragraph). The essay does nothing to back up the claim that the poem is effective. This is a poor essay. It really doesn't answer the question. (K.R.)

4. Kim

This is the best of the four in my view. The student has something to say about the poem and supports her reading with plenty of evidence. Not sure that I agree with her argument, but she puts it well. The idea that this poem offers a male-oriented world view is quite sophisticated. It is looking at the poem in a broader context than just words on the page. It also recognises the difference between the world-views of modern vs nineteenth century readers. The comments on original sin as an idea in the poem show that the student has some background knowledge about the historical period of the poem and is able to use it effectively. The discussion in para. 3 is especially good and shows a subtle reading of the ambiguity in the title. The comments on language in para. 4 are good – arguments are supported by evidence and explanation, though it's a little brief. The conclusion is fine, a mature personal response. (A.L.)

The teachers' marks

The four teachers were asked to give the essays a mark out of 10. Here are the results.

Essay	Teacher 1 (S.N)	Teacher 2 (A.N.)	Teacher 3 (K.R.)	Teacher 4 (A.L.)	Average Rank
1. Tan	7.5	7	6.5	8	2
2. Faysal	6	5	6	6.5	3
3. Veronika	4	4	2	3.5	4
4. Kim	8	8.5	8	9	1

Discussion

Discuss the teachers' comments, and the marks and rankings they arrived at. Do they agree with your evaluation of the essays? If not, what can you learn from their responses?

WRITING A CRITIQUE

There are three steps in writing a poetry critique, and all must be handled carefully for the critique to be successful. The steps are:

1. analysing the question or task;
2. reading and understanding the poem;
3. presenting your reading in a well-structured essay that uses appropriate language and techniques.

In the work that follows, you will learn about each of these steps in turn.

Step 1: Analysing the question

When you write about poetry you will often be given a question that your essay must answer. In this case, your first task should be to analyse the question, to find out exactly what is wanted. Every question contains *key words* that tell you what you must do in your essay.

Here are three typical questions that might be asked. Read each one, and think about what it asks readers to do.

1. Outline the main ideas in the poem, and show how these ideas are developed. Give your opinion of the poem's effectiveness.

2. State the main theme of the poem, and discuss how the structure and language of the poem shape the reader's response to the theme.

3. The poem offers an unusual view of love and romance. Discuss the portrayal of the lovers, and show how it differs from other 'love' poems you have studied. Say what effect this portrayal has had on your ideas about love poems.

Task words and topic words

Every question contains key words that indicate what has to be done. There are two types of key word. The first type are words which say what kind of action or thinking is required. You can think of these as *task words*. The second type are words which say what parts or aspects of the poem should be studied. You can think of these as *topic words*.

In this example, the *task words* have been underlined.

> <u>Outline</u> the main ideas in the poem, and <u>show how</u> these ideas are developed. <u>Give your opinion</u> of the poem's effectiveness.

Here the *topic words* have been underlined.

> Outline the <u>main ideas</u> in the poem, and show how these <u>ideas are developed</u>. Give your opinion of the poem's <u>effectiveness</u>.

Focussing on these key words gives a summary of what the question is asking:

> *Outline* the *main ideas* in the poem, and *show how* these *ideas are developed. Give* your *opinion* of the poem's *effectiveness.*

> That is: outline main ideas;
> show development;
> give opinion of effectiveness.

The first step in preparing to write a critique, then, is to find the task words and topic words in the question. This will help you to study the poem with the right purpose in mind.

Activity

1. Analyse questions 2 and 3 of the examples on page 110. For each question do the following.

    1. Underline the task words and topic words.
    2. Create your own brief summary of the question, using only the key words (as shown in the example above.)

2. Check your analysis of the question with others in your group or class.

Task words: what they mean

Printed below are some common task words, with explanations of their meanings.

Analyse	Show how a text or some part of it achieves its effects; that is, how it 'works'. Analysis of a poetic text involves examining basic elements such as sounds, structures, patterns and meanings. To be effective, an analysis of a text should also include a consideration of how it is read.
Argue	Make assertions about the topic, and back them up with explanations and examples. An argument is intended to persuade the reader to take a particular view. It tends to have a narrower focus than a discussion.
Comment	Make observations about some aspect of the poem, without necessarily giving an argument or a detailed explanation of how it works.
Compare (and contrast)	Discuss similarities and differences between poems, or between aspects of a poem.
Describe	Give a detailed account of features or ideas in the poem. It is useful to imagine writing for someone who hasn't read the poem, and who needs to be told enough about it to follow your comments.
Discuss	Examine from various angles, to arrive at an understanding. A discussion is usually a broad exploration of an issue, taking a variety of viewpoints into account.
Explain	Make clear how some aspect of the poem works, by giving the reader a detailed account of relationships, causes and effects.
Outline	Briefly describe some aspect of the poem, such as the main ideas or techniques, without going into lengthy or detailed discussion.

Topic words: some examples

Topic words refer to aspects of the poem that you may be asked to respond to. Topic words will vary from question to question, depending on the poem you are studying. You may be asked to focus on any of the following.

ideas	symbols	point of view
response	development	imagery
theme	language	tone
effectiveness	subject	and so on …
form	structure	

You should learn the meanings of these words and record them in a section of your notebook or file. You can add extra words to your list as you meet them in your studies.

Step 2: Reading the poem

You should do a careful reading of the poem before you begin planning your essay.

The first stage: working out a simple meaning

The first stage in reading the poem is to work out a 'basic' or simple meaning for the text. To do this you may have to:

- read the poem several times;
- look up the meaning of unfamiliar words;
- work out the subject and main ideas;
- jot down questions.

When reading the poem, you should pay careful attention to not only the words but also the layout and punctuation. Remember to read in sentences rather than focussing on single lines.

The second stage: reading for themes and effects

The second stage involves reading the poem in terms of themes and effects, to produce a more complex reading. This often means responding to the poem's ideas, situations and descriptions in a more 'philosophical' way. To do this you may have to:

- look for alternative ways of reading words and ideas;
- explore different word groups (nouns, verbs, adjectives);
- read the poem as a comment on life, society or people;
- reflect on your own experiences;
- draw on background information to help your construct your reading.

You should also consider the *aesthetics* of the poem – that is, the 'pleasing' qualities of the poem's design (for example, its use of sound, choice of words and artistic design).

A demonstration reading

The following pages will lead you through these steps using a specific poem, 'From the Lighthouse'. This poem was written in 1958 by Flora Podmore.

Read the poem by yourself before going on.

FROM THE LIGHTHOUSE

The nimbus has been growing since the dawn.
I know that warning well, and read the slow advance
Of angry squalls in pressing tide and turning wind,
And in the shrill confusion of the gulls.
Knowing more now than the radio can tell
(one more fair-weather friend)
I climb the stairs to check my light. Behind the glass
I flash an eye toward the dark horizon, and catching
Distant echoes of my fire in snapshot clouds,
Begin my preparations for the night.

The mechanism ticks the seconds off, and as
The sea turns black, I think how once again
By my own light the storm has tracked me to a hollow shell.
Below, the tethered dinghy bobs and tugs the pier, inviting me
To row ashore and spend the evening safe.
But in the darkened town another squall awaits,
Against whose gentle ravages my light has no defence.
Winter at sea and winter in the soul
Bring on the dark and pound against the shutters.
I'll set my will once more against the wind.

I bolt the storm doors as the squall sets in,
Withdraw into that vaulted inner room, and turn my back
Upon the outside world. The better to protect those
Distant lives whose claim upon me keeps me in my place.
The cold throat of the tower softly moans.
Here I will stay and wait,
And doing nothing, do what must be done
As those who live alone for others' sakes have always done.
I set my candle on a shelf, a tower tipped with light,
And with a puff of breath call on the darkness.

Flora Podmore

Writing on the poem

When reading poems for analysis, it can be helpful to annotate and paraphrase sections
of the text.

Annotate   means to make notes about parts of the poem, or mark out parts of
it by underlining and writing on the page where the poem is printed.

Paraphrase   means to translate parts of the poem into everyday language that
will help you to think about the ideas more clearly.

The following pages show how annotation and paraphrase can help clarify your reading. The
annotations on the poem are accompanied by written notes that show how ideas have
developed in one reader's mind.

Read through the annotations and notes, and work through the activities that accompany them.

First reading	Read several times.
	Read in sentences, not lines.
	Check meaning of key words.
	Annotate the text, noting questions.
	Work out subject and main ideas.

Subject matter: woman alone in a lighthouse, with storm approaching

① First part sets the scene: signs of storm, radio is silent, she is alone.

FROM THE LIGHTHOUSE

a type of storm cloud.

The nimbus has been growing since the dawn.

I know that warning well, and read the slow advance

Of angry squalls in pressing tide and turning wind,

And in the shrill confusion of the gulls.

Knowing more now than the radio can tell   *She knows more than the*

5 (one more fair-weather friend)   *radio news? Suggests experience, or radio off the air.*

I climb the stairs to check my light. Behind the glass

I flash an eye toward the dark horizon, and catching

Distant echoes of my fire in snapshot clouds,

10 Begin my preparations for the night.

② She thinks about previous storms. Considers going ashore but decides to stay.

Q: What is wrong in town?

The mechanism ticks the seconds off, and as

The sea turns black, I think how once again   *This has happened before – or something similar.*

By my own light the storm has tracked me to a hollow shell.

Below, the tethered dinghy bobs and tugs the pier, inviting me

15 To row ashore and spend the evening safe.   *What is this?*

But in the darkened town another squall awaits,

Against whose gentle ravages my light has no defence.

Winter at sea and winter in the soul   *Important comparison. Is the storm a metaphor?*

Bring on the dark and pound against the shutters.

20 I'll set my will once more against the wind.

③ She makes ready for the storm, comforted by thoughts of others who depend on her light.

I bolt the storm doors as the squall sets in,

Withdraw into that vaulted inner room, and turn my back

Upon the outside world. The better to protect those   *An unusual pause. mixed feelings?*

Distant lives whose claim upon me keeps me in my place.   *Sailors at sea?*

25 The cold throat of the tower softly moans.

Here I will stay and wait,

And doing nothing, do what must be done

As those who live alone for others' sakes have always done.   *} A sense of duty?*

I set my candle on a shelf, a tower tipped with light,

30 And with a puff of breath call on the darkness.   *| Blows out the candle?*

First reading

Read the annotations and notes that this reader has made, and discuss them in your group.

Summary notes

Subject and ideas

Poem involves a character in a lighthouse. It records the speaker's thoughts and reactions in response to an approaching storm. The character sees the signs of the approaching storm, and sets about making preparations. She considers going ashore to safety but decides to stay put out of a sense of duty. She thinks about storms in her life, and how people must weather the storms for the sake of others (or is it because of others?) She closes the doors, goes inside and waits for the storm to hit.

Technique

Poem is written in the first person (using "I"). This creates the impression that we are listening in to the character's thoughts (this is interior monologue). This technique is used to create a highly personal, thoughtful or philosophical tone.

Language

The vocabulary of the poem is fairly straightforward, though the word "nimbus" may be confusing. The dictionary explains that "nimbus" is a type of storm cloud:

> **nimbus** n. **1.** A bright cloud believed by ancient people to surround a god or saint. **2.** Any cloud or aura surrounding a person or object, especially in mythology. **3.** In art, a golden disc representing radiance about the head of divinity; a halo. **4.** A type of dense cloud with uneven edges, which brings heavy rain or snow; a storm cloud; (q.v. cumulo ~ packed, dark cloud; nimbostratus). **5.** In medicine, a subjective premonition of the onset of pathological symptoms such as migraine or mental disturbance.

The language is often emotive, and words are used to suggest a gloomy mood:
eg,   angry squall
         pressing tide
         sea turns black

Structure

The poem is in three parts, and each section explores a different topic.
        First stanza – signs of the coming storm.
        Second stanza – comparison of storms and life.
        Third stanza – reasons for facing the storm alone.

Questions

First reading opens up a number of questions:
        What is meant by "another squall" in the town?
        What is "winter in the soul"?
        What are items such as the storm and the lighthouse being used to represent?
        What happens at the end?

Activities

1. Make a list of other questions you have about the poem.

2. Is there another meaning of the word 'nimbus' that also fits the poem?

3. Look up the meanings of other words or phrases in the poem that seem important, or which you are uncertain about. The following are some suggestions:

    ravages ('gentle ravages'); **distant** ('distant lives'); **light** ('my light').

Second reading	Try alternative readings of words, phrases.
	Work out answers to your questions.
	Read poem as a comment on life, people, society.
	Apply background information.
	Judge aesthetics and overall effectiveness.

FROM THE LIGHTHOUSE

A warning or premonition ?

The nimbus has been growing since the dawn.

I know that warning well, and read the slow advance

Of angry squalls in pressing tide and turning wind,   *Suggests danger and betrayal.*

And in the shrill confusion of the gulls.

5 Knowing more now than the radio can tell   *More than it knows? More than it says? It cannot tell what she knows?*

one more fair-weather friend)

A friend who leaves in times of trouble, like others before.

I climb the stairs to check my light. Behind the glass

I flash an eye toward the dark horizon, and catching   *Her gaze, or the lighthouse beam?*

Distant echoes of my fire in snapshot clouds,   *The beam? Her anger? Her spirit ?*

10 Begin my preparations for the night.

The mechanism ticks the seconds off, and as   *The lighthouse machinery*

The sea turns black, I think how once again   *An ominous image*

By my own light the storm has tracked me to a hollow shell.   *She has no inner strength. The storm knows it, or causes it.*

Below, the tethered dinghy bobs and tugs the pier, inviting me

15 To row ashore and spend the evening safe.

But in the darkened town another squall awaits,   *some kind of personal trouble?*

Against whose gentle ravages my light has no defence.   *Contrasts with the 'angry squall' of the storm.*

Winter at sea and winter in the soul   *Her strength/spirit ?*

Bring on the dark and pound against the shutters.

20 I'll set my will once more against the wind.   *She goes against expectations?*

I bolt the storm doors as the squall sets in,   *Withdrawing into herself ?*

Withdraw into that vaulted inner room, and turn my back

Upon the outside world. The better to protect those   *Turns rejection into acceptance – duty.*   *Her previous 'lives'? Or, people who are distant and unfriendly ?*

Distant lives whose claim upon me keeps me in my place.   *Gives her a reason to be strong? Or imprisons her?*

25 The cold throat of the tower softly moans.

Here I will stay and wait,   *Candle and lighthouse both symbols for the woman? Life ?*

And doing nothing, do what must be done   *Those who sacrifice for others, or who are harmful to others ?*

As those who live alone for others' sakes have always done.

I set my candle on a shelf, a tower tipped with light,   *speaking, or blowing out the candle.*

30 And with a puff of breath call on the darkness.   *Death? Fear? Or SAFETY ?*

Second reading

Read the second set of annotations that the reader has made, and discuss these in your groups. See if you agree with the reading of words and phrases. If not, add your own comments.

Summary notes

Language

There are many double-meanings and ambiguous words:

title – suggests the speaker will not leave but always be speaking, observing *from* there?

nimbus – cloud, but can also mean early warning of an emotional upset or physical pain.

turning – suggests betrayal.

tell – can mean what the radio says, or the fact that it doesn't know her like a real friend.

eye/fire/light – refers to the lighthouse tower and the speaker's gaze or her life-force?

"hollow shell" – the tower, but also a feeling of fear or emptiness in the speaker?

another squall/ "winter in the soul" – emotional storms, relationship problems?

"set my will once more" – a last effort?

distant lives – sailors at sea, but also people who are emotionally distant, or even the speaker's own past "lives"?

keeps me in my place – helps the speaker stay strong, or holds her down? Unusual mid-line pause before "The better to protect …" suggests ambivalence – sense of duty or a justification for not risking contact with others?

"puff of breath" – frosty breath, or blowing out the candle (symbolism of candle?)

darkness – the storm? death? etc.

Mood & atmosphere

Poem creates a fairly bleak picture. Some aspects of nature are made lifelike as if they have a will of their own – the squalls are "angry" and the storm has "tracked" the speaker (personification). This creates a sinister feeling. There is also a sense of sadness created by references to betrayal and loss, eg. "one more fair-weather friend," and "gentle ravages".

Symbols

Some images seem symbolic. The lighthouse tower seems to symbolise a number of things: personal strength, but also the speaker herself, with her "hollow" centre and her "light". Bolting the storm doors suggests withdrawing from people or from the world. The lighted candle suggests "keeping the faith" or an act of hope, and the blowing out of the candle may signal either a loss of hope, or an acceptance of what is about to happen. Heart of the storm – peaceful refuge in the lighthouse? Could also be an emptiness?

Themes

Poem invites readers to make a comparison between stormy weather and upheavals in people's lives ("winter at sea and winter in the soul"). It seems to say that sometimes duty requires us to weather the storm for the sake of other people ("do what must be done … for others' sakes"). It is not clear if the speaker does this by choice or is forced by circumstances to face the storm alone. Or because she is afraid of contact with others?

Poem seems to portray people as having a combination of strength and hollowness, like the lighthouse tower – this emphasises the difference between appearing strong for others, but feeling weak or afraid.

It is not made clear what kind of troubles are represented by the weather. The character may be referring to a relationship that has soured; or to the fears of age and death; or to social problems she shares with other people – eg, the experiences of women in general?

Background

Flora Podmore often wrote about the experience of women in society, and women's issues. In the 1950s women were expected to lead lives of self-sacrifice. Is the poem a comment on women's role in society?

Step 3: Writing the critique

Once you have read the poem thoroughly it is time to write your critique. This is also best done in two stages.

The first stage involves making a plan; the second is the actual writing.

The first stage: making a plan

Critiques or critical essays have a typical structure, but the content will depend upon the poem you are studying and the question you have been given (if any).

A typical question will ask you to state the main ideas and themes of the poem, and to explain how these are developed.

(You may be told to focus on certain aspects of the poem, such as the language or the structure. If not, you should comment on those aspects that seem important in the particular poem.)

Look back to pages 104 and 110 for examples of fairly typical questions if you need to remind yourself of the kinds of critical essays that are required.

This diagram shows a common essay structure that may be a useful guide for your writing.

First paragraph –
gives an overview of the ideas and themes, and states the reader's view about the poem.

Middle paragraphs –
give a detailed explanation of how the ideas are developed and presented.
Each paragraph will deal with a separate aspect: eg, the argument, the language, the structure.
Main points are supported by examples.

Final paragraph –
is a brief summary of the main argument about the poem.

When planning your critique or critical essay, it is a good idea to map out your key points with this structure in mind.

On the next page is one reader's plan for an essay on Flora Podmore's poem, 'From the Lighthouse' using the notes from page 115 and page 117.

A sample plan

Main idea	Poem uses comparison between storms and personal upheavals to comment on life. It shows that what looks like strength of character may be a hollow sense of duty, or a way of withdrawing from the world. Is thought-provoking rather than descriptive.
Point 1	The argument is developed through character and situation. Explanation: Her thoughts focus on the link between weather and feelings; 1st person p.o.v. (point of view - internal monologue). Example: quote lines 12–13.
Point 2	Development of ideas is helped by language. Explanation: language triggers suitable emotions. Examples: "angry squall", "sea turns black" etc.
Point 3	Development of ideas is also helped by images and symbols. Explanation: objects and actions represent our responses to problems in life. Examples: lighthouse as tower of strength (but a hollow one); bolting doors as an image of withdrawing from the world.
Point 4	Poem's theme = strength in adversity. Is strength an inner quality or something forced on us when we have no escape? What is "strength"? Explanation: The extended comparisons between storm and personal troubles, and between tower and speaker raise questions about the individual and life generally. Example: lines 16–20.
Conclusion	A very philosophical poem, easy to read as a comment on life; can be read in a number of ways.

Each of these sections can be developed into a paragraph in the essay.

The second stage: writing the essay

Once the plan is finished, it is time to write up the essay. This may mean doing a number of drafts to ensure that both the ideas and the expression are polished.

Following are the opening paragraphs of an essay developed from the plan above. Read each one carefully, noting how the basic ideas in the plan have been developed.

Main idea	Poem uses comparison between storms and personal upheavals to comment on life. It shows that what looks like strength of character may be a hollow sense of duty, or a way of withdrawing from the world. Is thought-provoking rather than descriptive.

Flora Podmore's poem, "From the Lighthouse" offers a thought-provoking comment on the way we deal with problems in life. The poem tackles its subject by comparing personal problems with winter storms. As the speaker retreats into her lighthouse, the poem asks whether facing life alone is a form of strength, or a last resort for those who have been hurt too many times. It suggests that in life, as with the weather, we are often forced to face the storms alone.

Point 1:   The argument is developed through character and situation.
Explanation: Her thoughts focus on the link between weather and feelings; 1st person p.o.v. (internal monologue).
Examples: quote lines 12–13.

> The ideas in Podmore's poem are developed through a dramatic use of character and situation. The poem uses a first person point of view to report the thoughts of a character awaiting the arrival of a winter storm, which has been signalled by the building clouds, the "pressing tide" and the "turning wind" (l. 1–3). While she prepares for the storm's arrival, the character reflects on "winter at sea and winter in the soul" (l. 18). In this way, the reader is invited to think about this comparison and what it might teach us. The character in Podmore's poem cannot escape her circumstances. In the town she faces "another squall" (l. 16), suggesting that something in her past has forced this life of isolation. The choice to face the storm alone has been forced upon her. As readers, we are drawn into this situation by sympathising with the character's thoughts and actions; and so the poem leads us to ask questions about our own experiences.

Point 2:   Development of ideas is helped by language.
Explanation: language triggers suitable emotions.
Examples: angry squall, the sea turns black etc.

> The poem's language also contributes to its development of ideas. Many words and phrases invite emotional responses that create a depressing or threatening mood. This helps to create the pessimistic outlook of the poem. The ambiguous word "nimbus" (l. 1) suggests not only a build-up of cloud but also a kind of premonition. Phrases such as "pressing tide and turning wind" imply something persistent and threatening or treacherous. Some descriptions are straightforward, such as "the sea turns black" (l. 12); others are more complex and disturbing, such as "the storm has tracked me to a hollow shell" (l. 13). This image implies that the storm has a purpose in mind, and that it has been drawn to the tower and the speaker's inner emptiness. This mixture of simple and complex images adds depth to the poem by describing a situation that the reader can relate to on one level, but which is very ambiguous and unsettling on another.

Structuring the argument

These examples show how the paragraphs in the body of the essay are structured. Each begins with a clear statement about the poem. This is then explained in detail, with the help of quotations from the text.

Paragraph two (Point 1) shows this structure clearly.

> **Statement:** The ideas in Podmore's poem are developed through a dramatic use of character and situation.
>
> **Explanation & examples:** The poem uses a first person point of view to report the thoughts of a character awaiting the arrival of a winter storm, which has been signalled by the building clouds, the "pressing tide" and the "turning wind" (l. 1–3). While she prepares for the storm's arrival, the character reflects on "winter at sea and winter in the soul" (l. 18). In this way, the reader is invited to think about this comparison and what it might teach us. The character in Podmore's poem cannot escape her circumstances. In the town she faces "another squall" (l. 16), suggesting that something in her past has forced this life of isolation. The choice to face the storm alone has been forced upon her. As readers, we are drawn into this situation by sympathising with the character's thoughts and actions, and so the poem leads us to ask questions about our own experiences.

1. Use this structure to write the next paragraph in the essay, using the plan, and the notes from pages 115 and 117 as a guide. Remember to start with a clear statement, and then add the explanation. You will need to select examples and quotations to back up your statement.

   Point 3:   Development is also helped by images and symbols.
   Explanation: objects and actions represent our responses to problems in life.
   Examples: lighthouse as tower of strength (but a hollow one);
   bolting doors as an image of withdrawing from the world, etc.

   Your paragraph:

   Statement: _____

   Explanation & examples: _____

   _____

   _____

   _____

2. Read out your paragraph to others in your class or group, and discuss the way each person has developed the ideas in this part of the essay.

Aspects of style

The language and tone of your essay are important. You should write in a style that is suitable for adult readers. Even though your essay may be marked by your teacher, a good critique should be written with a broader readership in mind. This means using a 'formal' style.

You should note the following guidelines when writing your essay.

1. *Avoid casual expressions and slang terms.*

Instead of this:	Use this:	
maybe	perhaps, could be	
I reckon	I think, I believe	… and so on.

2. *Use the technical terms you have learned in your study of poetry.*

   These might include terms such as:

speaker	sound	metaphor	iambic pentameter
reader	associations	simile	stress
subject	connotations	symbol	tone
idea	stanza	description	personification
theme	rhythm	sound	alliteration
technique	rhyme	image	metre

3. *Make your key statements clear by using a direct style.*

   Help your reader by using phrases like these:

   The main idea of the poem is …
   The theme of the poem is …
   The theme is developed through …

4. *Make your evidence stand out by signalling explanations and examples clearly.*

> For example:
>
> An example of this is ...
> This can be seen in ...
> This effect is created by ...

5. *Use the correct referencing conventions to indicate quotations from the poem.*

> For example:
>
> Make your quotations accurate: check wording, spelling and punctuation.
>
> Use citation marks around quoted sections: "To be or not to be."
>
> Give line numbers in brackets after a quotation from a poem:
> "– yet / No one actually starves" (l. 19–20).
>
> Use a slash (/) to show line breaks:
> "The sea is calm tonight / The tide is full."
>
> Use ellipsis (...) to show sections left out of a quotation:
> "I leave the book ... watching boughs strain against the sky."

Activity

Finish writing the essay on 'From the Lighthouse,' paying attention to the structure of paragraphs and the style of the writing.

You can work from the existing plan or use your own.

The finishing touch: a title

Readers react more favourably to an essay that has an interesting title – especially if the title gives a clue to the argument. Titles such as "Essay on 'From the Lighthouse'" tend to be dull and uninviting.

Activity

Here is a selection of titles that you could use for your finished essay. Discuss with a partner or small group the strengths and weaknesses of each. Think about the title from the reader's point of view: which one would encourage you to read the essay?

1. 'Winter in the Soul': Reading Flora Podmore's 'From the Lighthouse'
2. The Theme of Sacrifice in 'From the Lighthouse'
3. The Main Ideas of 'From the Lighthouse'
4. 'Calling on the Darkness'
5. Image and Symbol in 'From the Lighthouse'
6. My Reading of 'From the Lighthouse'

You can use one of these titles to finish off the essay, or invent one of your own.

Poems for study

On pages 124 to 128 there are several more poems for you to read and discuss critically. Suggestions for reading are printed after the poems on page 129.

WRITING A POETRY CRITIQUE – SUMMARY SHEET

1. Analyse the question

Underline task words and topic words.
Summarise the requirements.

2. Read the poem

a. Read for a 'first' meaning.

Read several times.
Read in sentences, not lines.
Check meanings of key words.
Annotate the text, noting questions.
Work out subject and main ideas.

b. Read for themes and effects.

Explore word groups (nouns, verbs, adjectives).
Try out alternative readings of words, phrases.
Work out answers to your questions.
Read poem as a comment on life, people, society.
Apply background information.
Judge aesthetics.

3. Write the essay

a. Make a plan.

Consider the question.
Outline subject and themes.
Outline key points and examples.

b. Write the essay.

Focus on:
– clear argument;
– a key statement in each paragraph;
– examples from the text;
– correct quotation techniques.

c. Proof-read and polish.

Techniques for quotation

1. Use citation marks around quoted sections: "To be or not to be."
2. Quote accurately: use the exact words, spelling and punctuation:
   "Dost thou deny me, thus?"
3. Indicate line breaks with a slash: "The sea is calm tonight / The tide is full."
4. Give line numbers in brackets after a quotation: "Withdraw into that vaulted inner room, and turn my back / Upon the outside world" (l. 22–23).
5. Use ellipsis to indicate sections left out of a quotation:
   "I climb the stairs … Begin my preparations for the night."
6. Try to work the quotation into your sentence smoothly:
   Podmore uses the image of a gathering storm to develop her arguments about "winter in the soul" (l. 18).

MIRROR

I am silver and exact, I have no preconceptions.
Whatever I see I swallow immediately
Just as it is, unmisted by love or dislike.
I am not cruel, only truthful –
The eye of a little god, four-cornered.
Most of the time, I meditate on the opposite wall.
It is pink, with speckles. I have looked at it so long
I think it is part of my heart. But it flickers.
Faces and darkness separate us over and over.

Now I am a lake. A woman bends over me,
Searching my reaches for what she really is.
Then she turns to those liars, the candles or the moon.
I see her back, and reflect it faithfully.
She rewards me with tears and an agitation of hands.
I am important to her. She comes and goes.
Each morning it is her face that replaces the darkness.
In me she has drowned a young girl, and in me an old woman
Rises toward her day after day, like a terrible fish.

Sylvia Plath

ELEGY FOR DROWNED CHILDREN

What does he do with them all, the old king:
Having such a shining haul of boys in his sure net,
How does he keep them happy, lead them to forget
The world above, the aching air, birds, spring?

Tender and solicitous must be his care
For those whom he takes down into his kingdom one by one
– Why else would they be taken out of the sweet sun,
Drowning towards him, water plaiting their hair?

Unless he loved them deeply how could he withstand
The voices of parents calling, like birds by the water's edge,
By swimming-pool, sand bar, river-bank, rocky ledge,
The little heaps of clothes, the futures carefully planned.

Yet even an old acquisitive king must feel
Remorse poisoning his joy, since he allows
Particular boys each evening to arouse
From leaden-lidded sleep, softly to steal

Away to the whispering shore, there to plunge in,
And fluid as porpoises swim upward, upward through the dividing
Waters until, soon, each back home is striding
Over thresholds of welcome dreams with wet and moonlit skin.

Bruce Dawe

TOADS

Why should I let the toad *work*
  Squat on my life?
Can't I use my wit as a pitchfork
  And drive the brute off?

Six days of the week it soils
  With its sickening poison –
Just for paying a few bills!
  That's out of proportion.

Lots of folk live on their wits:
  Lecturers, lispers,
Losels, loblolly-men, louts –
  They don't end as paupers.

losel = worthless person;
loblolly-men = attendant to ship's surgeon

Lots of folk live up lanes
  With a fire in a bucket;
Eat windfalls and tinned sardines –
  They seem to like it.

Their nippers have got bare feet,
  Their unspeakable wives
Are skinny as whippets – and yet
  No one actually *starves*.

Ah, were I courageous enough
  To shout *Stuff your pension!*
But I know, all too well, that's the stuff
  That dreams are made on:

For something sufficiently toad-like
  Squats in me too;
Its hunkers are heavy as hard luck,
  And cold as snow,

And will never allow me to blarney
  My way to getting
The fame and the girl and the money
  All at one sitting.

I don't say, one bodies the other
  One's spiritual truth;
But I do say it's hard to lose either,
  When you have both.

Philip Larkin

THE HORSES

Barely a twelvemonth after
The seven days war that put the world to sleep,
Late in the evening the strange horses came.
By then we had made our covenant with silence,
But in the first few days it was so still
We listened to our breathing and were afraid.
On the second day
The radios failed; we turned the knobs; no answer.
On the third day a warship passed us, heading north,
Dead bodies piled on the deck. On the sixth day
A plane plunged over us into the sea. Thereafter
Nothing. The radios dumb;
And still they stand in corners of our kitchens,
And stand, perhaps, turned on, in a million rooms
All over the world. But now if they should speak,
If on a sudden they should speak again,
If on the stroke of noon a voice should speak,
We would not listen, would not let it bring
That old bad world that swallowed its children quick
At one great gulp. We would not have it again.
Sometimes we think of the nations lying asleep,
Curled blindly in impenetrable sorrow,
And then the thought confounds us with its strangeness.
The tractors lie about our fields; at evening
They look like dank sea monsters crouched and waiting.
We leave them where they are and let them rust:
'They'll moulder away and be like other loam.'
We make our oxen drag our rusty ploughs,
Long laid aside. We have gone back
Far past our fathers' land.
                    And then, that evening
Late in the summer the strange horses came.
We heard a distant tapping on the road,
A deepening drumming: it stopped, went on again
And at the corner changed to hollow thunder.
We saw the heads
Like a wild wave charging and were afraid.
We had sold our horses in our fathers' time
To buy new tractors. Now they were strange to us
As fabulous steeds set on an ancient shield
Or illustrations in a book of knights.
We did not dare go near them. Yet they waited,
Stubborn and shy, as if they had been sent
By an old command to find our whereabouts
And that long-lost archaic companionship.
In the first moment we had never a thought
That they were creatures to be owned and used.
Among them were some half a dozen colts
Dropped in some wilderness of the broken world,
Yet new as if they had come from their own Eden.
Since then they have pulled our ploughs and borne our loads,
But that free servitude still can pierce our hearts.
Our life is changed; their coming our beginning.

Edwin Muir

IN AN ARTIST'S STUDIO

One face looks out from all his canvasses,
  One selfsame figure sits or walks or leans:
  We found her hidden just behind those screens,
That mirror gave back all her loveliness.
A queen in opal or in ruby dress,
  A nameless girl in freshest summer-greens,
  A saint, an angel – every canvass means
The same one meaning, neither more nor less.
He feeds upon her face by day and night,
  And she with true kind eyes looks back on him,
Fair as the moon and joyful as the light:
  Not wan with waiting, not with sorrow dim;
Not as she is, but was when hope shone bright;
  Not as she is, but as she fills his dream.

Christina Rossetti

THINKING ABOUT HEAVEN

I lay, and thought about heaven.
I was eight. The ceiling offered no clue.
The problem was not: Am I going?
But: When I get there, what do I do?
    The show, they said, would run and run
Forever. That was my major fear.
However pleasant what you did there was
How would it feel in its millionth year?
    I could sense a nightmare coming on.
The principal task was to comprehend
How big heaven was in time and space
To size it up from end to end.
    I panicked when I saw an endless line
Of rods of time laid whitely in the gloom
Forever and forever; would not say amen
To that infinite horror in the room.
    The curtains flickered in the night.
Groaning, I prayed for sleep, which came.
Afterwards, they told me that eternal
And everlasting are not the same,
    That heaven is eternal, outside time,
Which measurement of years or miles cannot record.
Later, I had my appendix out
And got a notion of the great reward
    As a sort of anaesthetic
And Jesus as the surgeon with the knife.
This model served a stopgap purpose
Until the time came in my life
    When the problem didn't figure any more.
Heaven has receded, but earth designs
Equivalent dilemmas, and the ceiling still
Encodes its messages in cracks and lines.

John Richmond

I POET

ah was readin
readin all de time
fram book
fram play
fram t.v.
fram life
in odder words
fram yuh all
befo ah was writin
ah was readin
yuh all
neva did know who yuh all was but
ah was full a love
ah give it here
ah give it dere
neva see no harm
in a likkle share of
de warmes ting ah have
sista, bredda,
older, younger
neva matta
jus love like evrybody was preachin
ah was readin
ah was lovin
befo ah was writin

ah read all yuh poems
ah read all yuh plays
ah read all tea leaf, palm,
anyting wid a good story
even if it didn't always have
a happy endin
an evryting ah read ah say,
but how come I know dis story aready? or
I do dat yesterday
I see dat last night
I live troo dat
so I stap readin fi a while
jus befo I start writin
I stap evryting
jus fi a moment
an I sey, maybe, (I humble)
I sey, maybe
it was you readin me all de time
so doah I was well hurt inside
wen yuh all did sey
I wasn't no poet
I never mind
cause I sey
I was poet all de time
so I start write
an I tankful
to madda an fadda
dat ah did read an love firs
fah I know
when I writin
I poem
is you
all you

Jean 'Binta' Breeze

Suggestions for reading the poems

'Mirror', Sylvia Plath.

Sylvia Plath (1932–63) was an American poet. She suffered from depression for many years and finally took her own life. Plath's work has been championed by feminist scholars, who value the perspective on women's experience that can be read in her poetry. This poem presents the world from the point of view of a mirror. It may be interesting to compare the emotionless, flat commentary of the mirror with the apparently traumatic experiences of the woman who looks into the mirror. The poem might also be read as a comment on how the world views women.

'Elegy for Drowned Children', Bruce Dawe.

Bruce Dawe (1930–) is an Australian poet whose work has often been included for study on Australian school and university courses. Dawe's poems often deal with their subjects in a 'grand' or 'majestic' style. This poem, which deals with the tragedy of drowned children, is offered as an elegy – a poem of mourning, or a funeral song lamenting the dead. The 'king' referred to in the first line may be 'King Neptune' the mythological ruler of the undersea world. Dawe's work has sometimes been criticised for ignoring women. Readers may wish to discuss this poem's exclusive focus on boys, in spite of its title, which refers to 'children'.

'Toads', Philip Larkin.

Philip Larkin (1922–85), a British poet and novelist, worked as a librarian. He is often regarded as a very conservative writer (that is, one who is attached to values of the past). 'Toads' can be read as a frustrated attack on the necessity of work. There are two toads referred to in the poem: one is work itself, but what the other represents is less clear – cowardice, lack of imagination, laziness? The final section of the poem says something about the relationship between these two toads, and how they prevent the speaker from throwing off the drudgery of work.

'The Horses', Edwin Muir.

Edwin Muir (1887–1959) was a Scottish poet and novelist. He used psychoanalysis (a form of psychological therapy) as a stimulus for his writing. His poems are often said to have dream-like or mythological qualities. This poem can be read as a portrayal of nature's forgiveness to humans, following some cataclysmic event (perhaps a nuclear war). Readers might focus on the relationship between humans and horses, and what is meant by the horses offering themselves to be used by humans. Alternatively, it might be interesting to read the poem as a fantasy in which the poem represents humanity's *wish* to exploit nature without feeling guilty about it.

'In an Artist's Studio', Christina Rossetti.

Christina Rossetti (1830–94) was a British poet with a strong commitment to the High Anglican faith. Many of her poems have religious subjects or themes. Rossetti had a long relationship with the painter James Collinson, but her religious convictions led to a split. This poem, which is in the form of a sonnet, can be read as an oblique commentary on a relationship, where the participants are no longer present and all that remains is the artist's paintings. It can be seen as a comment on the way art seems to preserve the past. It might be interesting to compare the poem with Shakespeare's *Sonnet 18*, in which the poet promises to preserve his love's beauty in verse.

'Thinking about Heaven', John Richmond.

John Richmond (1951–) is a British poet. He has worked as a teacher and English advisor, and now is a Commissioning Editor of Schools Programs for Channel 4 Television in London. He has written several poems about his religious upbringing which he says involved him as a child in much bible reading and brooding on spiritual matters. He describes himself now as having no organised faith but as still intrigued by the possibility of realities in the universe other than this one.

'I Poet', Jean 'Binta' Breeze.

Jean 'Binta' Breeze (1956–) was born in Jamaica. She studied acting and directing, taught English and Drama, and also worked for the Jamaican Cultural Development Commission. She moved to London in 1985, where she began performing her poetry, which is influenced by the rhythms of 'dub' music. This is a poem about being a poet. It can be read as an autobiographical account of the writer's struggle for acceptance. It can be also read as a comment on the relationship between poetry and the poet's life.

6.

Theories and Practices

WAITING

Night – and once again
while I wait for you, cold wind
turns into rain.

Shiki

THEORIES OF POETRY

One of the things that can make poetry study confusing is that ideas about poetry – what it is, what value it has, and so on – change over time, and from place to place. Philosophers, critics and poets themselves have developed many theories about what poetry is or should be, none of which has gained universal acceptance. The same is true of actual poetic practices – ways of writing and reading poetry. Each age and society produces its own forms of poetry, with particular rules and standards.

Finding out about these different views and forms of poetry from the past can help us to look at the ideas and practices of the present in a new way.

Activity

The table below sets out four different time periods, alongside columns for recording *ideas* or ways of thinking about poetry, and *forms* of poetry. Fill in the table by choosing from the items listed below it, matching up the columns in the way you think makes the best sense. You may have to guess most of the answers, but you should try to think of reasons for the choices you make. You might find it easiest to begin by thinking about 'Significant forms of poetry' for each time and place. (You will learn the 'right' answers in the work that follows.)

Time/Place	Ideas about poetry		Significant forms of poetry
	Its nature	Its value	
Greece 400 BC			
England 1800s			
USA & England 1950s			
Europe 1970s & 1980s			

Ideas about poetry

Its nature:
    an 'inspired' set of writings
    an imitation of life
    a dramatic portrayal of events and people
    an anonymous artwork
    an 'effect' produced by readers
    a dramatic portrayal of events and people
    a poet's personal feelings
    an unoriginal set of borrowed phrases

Its value:
    a dangerous influence
    a civilising influence
    an irrelevance
    a force for social change
    a source of meaning for society
    a source of moral lessons

Significant forms of poetry:
    dramatic verses, about historic people and events
    poems made up of 'random' lines of text
    strict form poems with strong 'personal' themes
    free verse, dealing with everyday objects and events

Discuss your decisions with others in the class, and give the reasons for the choices.

Four views of poetry

In this section you will study four ways of thinking about poetry that have been influential in shaping modern Western ideas. This is a small sample of the many arguments that have been advanced.

1. The Classical view

Plato: the poem as an 'Imitation of Life'

In Ancient Greece, over 2,000 years ago, 'poetry' meant dramatic portrayals of historic events and people. Poems may have been recited by storytellers (such as Homer), or presented on stage as plays (as was the case with works by Euripides and others).

Poets were thought to be inspired by Muses – goddesses who gave a poet special insight and gifts of expression. Here the Greek poet Homer calls upon the Muse to help him tell the story of the *Iliad*, which concerns the Trojan war and the actions of figures such as Achilles:

> Of the wrath of the son of Peleus – Of Achilles – Goddess, sing!
> That ruinous wrath that brought sorrows past numbering
> Upon the host of Achaea, and to Hades cast away
> the valiant souls of heroes ...

In Greek society, poetry was widely valued for its ability to teach moral lessons. In Homer's epic poem *The Odyssey*, for example, the character of Odysseus is presented as a hero who is sometimes too proud of his achievements. After blinding a cyclops who has threatened to eat his men, Odysseus taunts his foe while sailing away to safety:

> Cyclops, if any man of mortal birth
> Note thine unseemly blindness, and inquire
> The occasion, tell him that Laertes' son,
> Odysseus, the destroyer of walled cities
> Whose home is Ithaca, put out thine eye.

Odysseus' pride almost gets his crew killed when the enraged cyclops hurls a boulder at the ship, and his proud boasts result in other misfortunes for his men on their journey home. Through stories about characters like Odysseus, the poets played a role in teaching values and providing moral lessons.

In spite of the importance given to poetry in Greek cultural life, there was nevertheless much debate about its nature and value. A significant figure in these debates was Plato (427–347BC), a philosopher who lived in Athens. Plato wrote many influential works on topics such as politics, literature and ethics. His most famous book, *The Republic*, described what the ideal society should be like.

Plato had a different view of poetry from others of his time. He believed that poets acquired a form of madness when influenced by the Muses, and that they could therefore not be trusted to teach people what was true and good.

In the extract from *The Republic* on the next page Plato presents his argument about the place of poetry in society. The argument is in the form of a conversation between two characters, Socrates and Glaucon.

Read through the dialogue, then do the activities that follow.

Studying Poetry

from The Republic (366BC)   *Plato*

Socrates:	Of the many excellences which I perceive in the order of our state, there is none which pleases me better than the rule about poetry.
Glaucon:	To what do you refer?
Socrates:	To the rejection of imitative poetry, which certainly ought not to be received.
Glaucon:	What do you mean?
Socrates:	That all poetical imitations are ruinous to the understanding of the hearers,and that the knowledge of their true natures is the only antidote to them.
Glaucon:	Explain your remark.
Socrates:	Let us take any common instance. There are beds and tables in the world – plenty of them, are there not?
Glaucon:	Yes.
Socrates:	But there are only two Ideas or Forms of them – one the idea of a bed, the other of a table.
Glaucon:	True.
Socrates:	And the maker of either of them makes a bed or table for our use in accordance with the Idea, but no-one makes the ideas himself – how could he?
Glaucon:	Impossible.
Socrates:	And there is another artist who is the maker of all the works of all the other workmen.
Glaucon:	What an extraordinary man!
Socrates:	Oh, you are incredulous, are you? Do you see that there is a way in which you could make all these things yourself?
Glaucon:	What way?
Socrates:	None quicker than that of turning a mirror round and round – you would soon enough make the sun and the heavens, and the earth and yourself, and all the things of which we were just now speaking, in the mirror.
Glaucon:	Yes, but they would be appearances only.
Socrates:	Very good, you are coming to the point now. And the painter, too, is just such another – a creator of appearances, is he not?
Glaucon:	Of course.
Socrates:	Beds, then, are of the three kinds, and there are three artists who superintend them: God, the maker of the bed, and the painter. God made one bed in nature, and only one. And what shall we say of the carpenter – is he not also the maker of the bed?
Glaucon:	Yes.
Socrates:	But would you call the painter a creator and maker?
Glaucon:	Certainly not: he is the imitator of that which the others make.
Socrates:	Then you call him who is in third descent from nature an imitator?
Glaucon:	Certainly.
Socrates:	And the tragic poet is an imitator, and therefore, like all other imitators, he is thrice removed from the truth.

The following list summarises the key points of Plato's argument about poetry, but the statements are not in logical order. Using the above dialogue and notes as a guide, put the statements into a more effective order. (You can do this by numbering the statements from 1 to 6. The first statement has been numbered for you.)

	Therefore poetry cannot be trusted to represent Truth.
	The world of objects and actions is a reflection of the world of Ideas.
1	There are Ultimate Truths in nature.
	Human beings can come to know Truths of nature, in the form of Ideas.
	Poetry offers imitations that are 'thrice removed' from Truth.
	Poetry is an imitation of the world of objects and actions, not the world of Ideas.

Compare your ordering of the statements with the order of others in your class.

Aristotle: a reply to Plato

Many writers and critics have tried to argue against Plato's attack on poetry. Aristotle (384–322BC), another Greek philosopher (and a student of Plato), agreed that poetry was imitative, but he argued that this fact alone was no reason to condemn it. Through imitation, he said, people were both entertained and educated. For Aristotle, the issue was not 'Ultimate Truth', but how effective a poem was in teaching a moral principle.

Aristotle also argued that fictional representations of life gave people the chance to release their destructive emotions in a harmless context. This argument is still used today – for example, by people who argue that violent movies offer a harmless release of the audience's violent impulses. Aristotle called this 'harmless release' *catharsis*.

Aristotle set out his views in a number of works, the most famous being the *Poetics*. The following short extract contains his reply to Plato's arguments. As you read it, consider the following questions.

> On what points does Aristotle agree with Plato?
> On what points does he disagree?

---

from the Poetics (330BC)   *Aristotle*

Epic poetry and Tragedy, and Comedy also, are all in their general conception modes of imitation. Poetry in general seems to have sprung from two causes, each of them lying deep within our nature. First, the instinct of imitation is implanted in man from childhood. Through imitation he learns his earliest lessons and gains a natural pleasure from things imitated. Imitation, then, is one instinct in our nature. Next, there is the instinct for harmony and rhythm. Persons starting with this natural gift developed by degrees their special aptitudes, and this gave birth to poetry ...

The poet being an imitator, like a painter or any other artist, must of necessity imitate one of three objects – things as they were or are; things as they are said or thought to be; or things as they ought to be. Within the art of poetry itself there are two kinds of faults. If a poet describes the impossible, he is guilty of an error; but the error may be justified if the end of the art be thereby attained. Further, if the description is not true to fact, the poet may perhaps reply 'But this is as things *ought* to be'. In this way the objection may be met. If, however, the representation be of neither kind, the poet may answer, 'This is how men *say* the thing is'. This applies for example to tales about the gods.

In examining whether what has been said or done by a poet is poetically right or not, we must not look merely to the particular act or saying, and ask if it is good or bad. We must also consider by whom it is said or done, to whom, when, in whose interest, or for what end – whether, for instance it be to secure a greater good or avert a greater evil.

This list summarises the key points in Aristotle's argument about poetry. Put the statements into a more effective order by numbering them from 1 to 6. (The first statement has been numbered for you.)

	Poetry is therefore a natural and acceptable activity.
1	The urge to imitate is part of human nature.
	Poets may present things as they are or as they *should* be.
	False imitations may be forgiven if they make a more effective poem.
	Poetry is imitation in rhythmical form.
	Love of rhythm is part of human nature.

Compare your result with others in your class.

Theory and criticism

These discussions are dealing with questions of 'theory' – arguments about poetry in general, rather than about specific texts. This is different from 'criticism', which is the practice of analysing and evaluating specific works of literature.

In the work that follows you will encounter other theoretical arguments. Some of them may lead you to question or reshape your own developing theory about poetry – its 'nature' and value.

The Neoclassical view

The ideas of Plato, Aristotle and the other classical Greek writers were strong influences on Western thought for centuries. Translated from Greek into Latin, Aristotle's works spread through Europe, the Middle East and then to Britain, influencing generations of scholars who variously praised or condemned them. In the late 1700s in England, the writings became so popular (perhaps fuelled by news of archaeological discoveries in Greece and Rome) that the period came to be known as the neo-classical (meaning 'new-classical') period.

Samuel Johnson (1709–1784), a scholar known for his critical writings, and for producing the *Dictionary*, was strongly influenced by classical ideas. In 1765 he edited a collection of Shakespeare's plays, and set out his own views of poetry in the preface.

from Preface to Shakespeare (1765)   *Samuel Johnson*

Nothing can please many, and please for long, but just representations of nature. Shakespeare is above all writers, at least above all modern writers, the poet of nature; the poet that holds up to his readers a faithful mirror of manners and of life. His characters are not modified by the customs of particular places; ... they are the genuine progeny of common humanity, such as the world will always supply, and observations will always find ...

Shakespeare with his excellences has likewise many faults, and faults sufficient enough to obscure and overwhelm any other merit. His first defect is that ... he sacrifices virtue to convenience, and is so much more careful to please than to instruct, that he seems to write without any moral purpose. He makes no just distribution of good or evil, nor is he always careful to show in the virtuous a condemnation of the wicked; he carries his persons indifferently through right and wrong, and at the close dismisses them without further care, and leaves their examples to operate by chance. This is a fault the barbarity of his age cannot excuse; for it is always a writer's duty to make the world better, and justice is a virtue independent of time and place.

The emphasis on imitation and moral instruction in this piece by Samuel Johnson shows a 'classical' belief in the relationship between poetry and 'life' that is still held by many people today.

1. Consider, for example, the extract below which is taken from a review of a recently published novel.

> The novel's chief power lies in its ability to be re-interpreted for any age. Indeed, its main themes – the quest for truth, the intellectual 'poverty' of bigotry and the need for tolerance – are universal. However, as thematically rich as this novel is, it is above all the characters, their flawed complexity, and their situations that will engage the reader ... Put simply, they are as recognisable as the people we all know and the problems we all must face ...

What examples of a 'classical' belief in the relationship between literature and life can you find in this extract?

2. Collect a selection of reviews (about movies, books, music, poetry) from newspapers and magazines. How many of the reviewers use 'accurate imitation of life' and 'moral instruction' as measures of artistic worth?

An emphasis on 'accurate imitation of life' may be signalled by words such as:

    'believable',
    'true-to-life'
    'convincing'
    'lifelike'
    'realistic'
    and so on.

References to 'moral instruction' might take the form of praise or criticism that a text is:

    'enriching'
    'dangerous'
    'sexist'
    'valuable'
    'inspiring'
    'uplifting'
    'homophobic'
    'anti-racist'
    and so on.

3. Share your findings with others in your class. What do your findings suggests about the influence of classical ideas in the modern world?

(Note: Keep your copies of reviews as you will be asked to refer to them again later in the chapter.)

2. The Romantic view

William Wordsworth: the poem as 'Expressed Emotion'

At the start of the nineteenth century in England, the classical view of poetry was being challenged. The effects of industrialisation and the growth of cities led some writers to fear that human sensitivity and a love of nature was being lost through mechanisation and commercialism. This led them to focus on human emotions and individual experiences of nature, rather than epic stories of historical events and people.

William Wordsworth (1770–1850) was influential in establishing this 'Romantic' view of poetry. Wordsworth believed the best poetry recorded a poet's feelings about some experience. In the Preface to a collection of his poems, titled *Lyrical Ballads*, Wordsworth explained at length his ideas about what poetry was, and what a good poem should be like.

This extract from the preface contains Wordsworth's definition of poetry and his account of how poets compose their works.

---

from the Preface to Lyrical Ballads (1800)   *William Wordsworth*

What is a poet? ... He is a man speaking to men: a man, it is true, endowed with a more lively sensibility, more enthusiasm and tenderness, who has a greater knowledge of human nature, and a more comprehensive soul, than are supposed to be common among mankind; a man pleased with his own passions and volitions, and who rejoices more than other men in the spirit of life that is in him ... To these qualities he has added a disposition to be affected more than other men by absent things as if they were present ...

... poetry is the spontaneous overflow of powerful feelings: it takes its origin from emotion recollected in tranquillity: the emotion is contemplated till, by a species of reaction, the tranquillity gradually disappears, and an emotion kindred to that which was before the subject of contemplation, is gradually reproduced, and does itself actually exist in the mind. In this mood successful composition generally begins, and in a mood similar to this it is carried on; but the emotion, of whatever kind, and in whatever degree, from various causes, is qualified by various pleasures, so that in describing any passions whatsoever, which are voluntarily described, the mind will, upon the whole, be in a state of enjoyment.

Activity

Check your understanding of Wordsworth's argument by ticking those statements below that are most in agreement with his position.

☐   Every person has the capacity to write good poetry.

☐   A poet is more sensitive than the ordinary person.

☐   Poetry offers readers a direct description of the world.

☐   Poetry offers readers the poet's impression of the world.

☐   Quiet reflection is essential for the creation of poetry.

☐   Poets write according to strict rules of style and content.

☐   Poets write from 'within', following their own feelings.

Compare your decisions with the choices made by others in your class.

The poet's experience

The following poem, 'I Wandered Lonely as a Cloud,' is often cited as an example of the Romantic style in poetry.

Read the poem with the following question in mind.

> How do the content and style of the poem match Wordsworth's beliefs about 'good' poetry?

I WANDERED LONELY AS A CLOUD

I wandered lonely as a cloud
That floats on high o'er vales and hills,
When all at once I saw a crowd,
A host of golden daffodils;
Beside the lake, beneath the trees,
Fluttering and dancing in the breeze.

Continuous as the stars that shine
And twinkle in the milky way,
They stretched in never-ending line
Along the margin of a bay:
Ten thousand saw I at a glance,
Tossing their heads in sprightly dance.

The waves beside them danced; but they
Outdid the sparkling waves in glee;
A poet could not be but gay,
In such a jocund company;
I gazed – and gazed – but little thought
What wealth the show to me had brought:

For oft, when on my couch I lie
In vacant or in pensive mood,
They flash upon that inward eye
Which is the bliss of solitude;
And then my heart with pleasure fills,
And dances with the daffodils.

William Wordsworth

Activities

Listed on the next page are some features we can note about the poem. Many of these features are in accord with Wordsworth's 'Romantic' approach to poetry, as set out in his comments in the preface on page 137.

1. Fill in the table by explaining how each aspect of the poem fits into the Romantic model of poetry. The first example has been done for you. You will need to refer back to the poem, the 'Preface', and the introductory notes on page 137 to fill in the others.

Features	Romantic approach
The poem is written in the first person (using 'I').	Shows the valuing of personal experience, individualism.
The character in the poem is also a poet.	
The poem depicts the beauty of nature.	
There is an emphasis on an emotional response to nature.	
The language is simple and direct.	
The speaker reflects on the experience later.	

2. Wordsworth's ideas about poetry are still held by many people today; they are often taught as fact in poetry classes. There are a number of possible reasons for this, including the following.

   a. Romantic ideas were dominant when mass schooling was introduced, in the late 1800s, and became part of the way poetry was taught.

   b. Modern society (through consumerism, and through its faith in democracy) maintains a strong belief in the individual and individual experience.

   c. During the 1960s there was revival of belief in the value of personal experience, through the 'hippie' movement.

   d. In modern societies there is a growing distrust of science, leading to a new acceptance of religious and mystical views of the world.

   Which of these ideas do you find most convincing? Can you think of other reasons why Romanticism is still strong today?

3. Go back to the reviews you collected for the previous section. Do some of these reviews make use of Romantic values in their judgements? (These values and beliefs might be signalled by references to writers, directors and musicians as 'creators', and through references to 'sensitivity', 'expression', 'personal vision', and so on.)

   Are there examples where Romantic *and* Classical values (see page 132) are evident in the same review?

3. The New Critical view

Wimsatt & Beardsley: the poem as 'Artistic Object'

The great popularity of the Romantic view of poetry led many critics and readers to become fascinated by the lives of the poets themselves. If poetry was an expression of the poet's personal experience, it seemed logical to find out as much as possible about the poet's life and attitudes, and to use this as a way of understanding the poem. Students were taught to ask, 'What is the poet saying?' 'Why might he/she say that?' as if the poem were a piece of personal communication from the writer.

By the middle of the 20th century, some critics had become alarmed by this practice. They believed that the poems themselves were being ignored, and that poetry study had become a kind of popularity contest or a form of hero worship. They sought to make criticism more 'objective' and 'scientific' by focussing on what was written on the page, rather than guessing about the writer's intention or feelings. This view was strongly influenced by the growing prestige of science and technology during and after the Second World War.

In this extract from an essay titled, 'The Intentional Fallacy', two professors at Yale University, William Wimsatt (1907–75) and Monroe Beardsley (1915–), put the case for a more 'rigorous' reading of the words on the page. This was a key argument in shaping what came to be called 'New Criticism'.

---

from 'The Intentional Fallacy' (1958)   *W.K. Wimsatt & Monroe C. Beardsley*

We begin our discussion with a series of propositions summarised and abstracted to a degree where they seem to us axiomatic.

1.   A poem does not come into existence by accident ... Yet to insist on the designing intellect as a cause of a poem is not to grant design or intention a standard by which the critic is to judge the worth of a poet's performance.

2.   One must ask how the critic expects to get an answer to the question about intention. How is he to find out about what the poet tried to do? If the poet succeeded in doing it, then the poem itself shows what he was trying to do.

3.   Judging a poem is like judging a pudding or a machine. One demands that it work. It is only because an artifact works that we infer the intention of an artificer. 'A poem should not mean but be.' A poem can be only through its meaning – since its medium is words – yet it is, simply is, in the sense that we have no excuse for inquiring what part is intended or meant.

The poem is not the critic's own, and not the author's (it is detached from the author at birth and goes about the world beyond his power to intend about it or control it). The poem belongs to the public. It is embodied in language, the peculiar possession of the public, and it is about the human being, an object of public knowledge.

Activity

Wimsatt and Beardsley's argument can be summed up with these statements. Put the statements into a more effective order by numbering them from 1 to 6. (The first statement has been numbered for you.)

	Therefore, we should focus on what the poem actually says, not the poet's 'intention'.
	Once the poem is written and published, it becomes a public document.
	The meaning of a poem arises from the language within it – not from an outside source.
1	Poets may write for many reasons: personal, practical, political.
	Poets put forward their ideas in a public form, using public language.
	Readers should be able to get the meaning by focussing on the language of the poem.

A New Critical reading

Like all theories, New Criticism suits some kinds of poetry better than others. The New Critics were most impressed by poetry that seemed to 'stand on its own'. They valued poems which could be read on a number of levels, and which had complex structures and a 'rich' use of language. They believed such poems worked like complicated machines or living organisms, in which each part has an important function.

The work of American poet Robert Frost was praised by the New Critics. Frost's poems frequently offer the reader mini-dramas, with characters and plot, almost like a stage play. They can be read as stories or parables rather than as the expression of the poet's inner feelings.

Read the following poem, then work through the activities that follow.

'OUT, OUT –'

The buzz saw snarled and rattled in the yard
And made dust and dropped stove-length sticks of wood,
Sweet-scented stuff when the breeze drew across it.
And from there those that lifted eyes could count
Five mountain ranges one behind the other
Under the sunset far into Vermont.
And the saw snarled and rattled, snarled and rattled,
As it ran light, or had to bear a load.
And nothing happened: day was all but done.
Call it a day, I wish they might have said
To please the boy by giving him the half hour
That a boy counts so much when saved from work.
His sister stood beside them in her apron
To tell them 'Supper'. At the word, the saw,
As if to prove saws knew what supper meant
Leaped out at the boy's hand, or seemed to leap –
He must have given the hand. However it was,
Neither refused the meeting. But the hand!
The boy's first outcry was a rueful laugh,
As he swung toward them holding up the hand
Half in appeal, but half as if to keep
The life from spilling. Then the boy saw all –
Since he was old enough to know, big boy
Doing a man's work, though a child at heart –
He saw all spoiled. 'Don't let him cut my hand off –
The doctor, when he comes. Don't let him sister!'
So. But the hand was gone already.
The doctor put him in the dark of ether.
He lay and puffed his lips out with his breath.
And then – the watcher at his pulse took fright.
No one believed. They listened at his heart.
Little – less – nothing! – and that ended it.
No more to build on there. And they, since they
Were not the one dead, turned to their affairs.

Robert Frost

Activities

1. Imagine that you were going to present this poem as a stage play. Look through the poem for clues as to how you would set your stage (ie, what would you place in the foreground; what would be in the background; what other details could be included?). Then sketch the scene as it would appear to the audience. Compare sketches with others in your class.

   Which critics and theorists you have read would praise Frost's poem for its dramatic nature? What reasons would they give for their praise?

2. Some elements in the poem can be read as symbols that give additional meaning to the story. Match the symbols in the left hand column with the possible readings on the right.

Symbols	Readings
Setting sun	Represents technology with all its dangers.
Five mountain ranges	Represents the end of a cycle, and end of life.
The rural setting	Represents the permanence of nature, and vast periods of time.
The buzz saw	Represents the harmony of nature and humanity.
The boy	Represents innocent human life.

   Add any other symbols in the text to your list, and suggest their possible meanings.

   Compare the use of symbolism in 'Out Out –' to the more personal focus of Wordsworth's poem. How does this affect the complexity of each text?

Making connections

The title of Frost's poem is presented as a quotation. Many critics have suggested that the quotation comes from Shakespeare's play *Macbeth*. This suggests that we can make an *intertextual* connection between the poem and the play.

Toward the end of the play, just as he is about to face his enemies in combat, Macbeth hears the news that his wife, the Queen, has been killed. The following is Macbeth's response.

SEYTON   The Queen, my lord, is dead.

MACBETH   She should have died hereafter:
There would have been a time for such a word.
Tomorrow, and tomorrow and tomorrow
Creeps in this petty pace from day to day
To the last syllable of recorded time,
And all our yesterdays have lighted fools
The way to dusty death. Out, out, brief candle!
Life's but a walking shadow, a poor player
That struts and frets his hour upon the stage
And then is heard no more. It is a tale
Told by an idiot, full of sound and fury
Signifying nothing.

Connecting metaphors?

The last six lines of Macbeth's speech printed on the previous page contain a series of metaphors about life.

Macbeth compares life to: a candle that burns out;
      a shadow;
      a poor actor who makes one brief appearance;
      a pointless story, full of sound but without meaning.

Activities

1. Discuss how the *allusion* to these lines from *Macbeth* might influence the reading of Frost's poem. The following are some possible effects of reading the two texts side by side.

   a. The poem becomes a general comment on the futility of life.

   b. The poem becomes a story illustrating the heroic aspects of life.

   c. The poem becomes part of a 'literary tradition'.

2. The structure of 'Out Out-' can be read as a set of *oppositions*, like these.

Oppositions	
Nature	Technology
Nature's time (long)	Human time (short)
Cycles	A single event
Permanence	Impermanence

   Can you add others to the list?

3. Although these appear to be opposites, the poem can be read in a way that brings the two sides into harmony. Which of the following readings seems to achieve this?

   a. Because they are so insensitive to death, people can be viewed as animals, and so are a part of nature.

   b. While individual lives come and go, humanity itself lives on as part of nature.

   c. People understand that life is meaningless, but human nature helps them to triumph over adversity.

Discussion

Do these activities convince you that poems can be read in complex ways *without* the need to consider the poet's intentions and feelings? Is this the same as arguing that the poem alone is sufficient to make meaning?

You could discuss this question with others in your class, or stage a debate on the topic:

'Are words on the page all we need to make sense of a poem?'

4. A Post-Structural view

Roland Barthes: the poem as 'Open Text'

The New Critical approach to poetry argued that readers could always find the meaning of a poem by paying close attention to 'the words on the page'. This assumed that a text had a 'single' meaning, or a narrow range of meanings, that was 'fixed' by its language and structure – and that readers should all agree on what that meaning was.

In the late 1960s a number of philosophers and writers, mostly working in France, began to challenge the idea that texts had fixed, singular meanings. The French theorists argued that words always had the potential to be read in multiple ways, and that there were no absolute rules for deciding which meanings were correct. Attempts to impose 'objective' limits on the meanings of a text were dishonest they said. This didn't mean texts had no meanings, or that they could be made to mean just anything at all. It meant that the meanings people found 'in' texts were actually produced through the reading practices they used. A different practice would produce a different reading – which raised the question: Why were some practices taught rather than others?

Roland Barthes (1915–1980) was a key figure in what came to be known as the 'post-structuralist' movement (named because it followed the 'structuralist' movement, which focussed on analysing the codes and rules of texts). In this extract, adapted from one of his essays, Barthes sets out some of the post-structural ideas about literary texts.

---

from 'The Death of the Author' (1968)   *Roland Barthes*

A text is not a line of words, releasing a single meaning (the 'message' of the Author-God), but a space in which a variety of writings, none of them original, blend and clash. The text is a tissue of quotations drawn from the innumerable centres of culture. The writer can only imitate a gesture that is always anterior ... his only power is to mix writings. Did he wish to express himself, he ought at least to know that the inner thing he thinks to express is itself only a ready-formed dictionary.

Once the Author is removed, the claim to decipher a text becomes quite futile. In the multiplicity of writing, everything is to be *disentangled*, nothing deciphered; the structure can be followed, 'run' (like the thread of a stocking) at every point and at every level, but there is nothing beneath.

The reader is the space on which all the quotations that make up a writing are inscribed without any of them being lost; a text's unity lies not in its origin, but in its destination. Yet this destination cannot any longer be personal: the reader is without history, biography, psychology: he is simply that someone who holds together all the traces by which the text is constituted. Classic criticism has never paid any attention to the reader; for it, the writer is the only person in literature. We are now beginning to let ourselves be fooled no longer ... it is necessary to overthrow the myth: the birth of the reader must be at the cost of the death of the Author.

Activity

Post-structural views of literature are very complex and draw on understandings about language, culture, and psychology, but this extract from Barthes provides a glimpse of some key assumptions. See if you can re-construct Barthes' argument from these statements.

	Texts can therefore be read, or used, in different ways.
	The ways in which readers use texts can change over time.
	Meanings arise only from the social use of language.
	Texts, as objects made of language, have no fixed meanings.
	The meanings of texts are fixed only by readers.
1	Language contains no inherent meanings.

Reading as 'writing'

Post-structural theories questioned the common-sense distinction between reading and writing. They argued that every reading of a text was a form of 're-writing' because it was only through the process of reading that the meanings of a text became temporarily fixed. (You may have demonstrated this in class by showing how different oral presentations of a poem can change its meaning dramatically.)

Post-structuralists saw *all* texts as 'open' to an extent – that is, as having the potential to be read in various ways. But they most liked texts in which this openness was strongly signalled.

The following poem is an example of such a text. It is by Bob Perelman, a modern American poet. You may need to read it a number of times before doing the activities that follow.

CHINA

We live on the third world from the sun. Number three.
Nobody tells us what to do.
The people who taught us to count were being very kind.
It's always time to leave.
If it rains, you either have your umbrella or you don't.
The wind blows your hat off.
The sun rises also.
I'd rather the stars didn't describe us to each other;
    I'd rather we do it for ourselves.
Run in front of your shadow.
A sister who points to the sky at least once a decade is a good sister.
The landscape is motorized.
The train takes you where it goes.
Bridges among water.
Folks straggling along vast stretches of concrete,
    heading into the plane.
Don't forget what your hat and shoes will look like when you are
    nowhere to be found.
Even the words floating in the air make blue shadows.
If it tastes good we eat it.
The leaves are falling. Point things out.
Pick up the right things.
Hey guess what? What? *I've learned how to talk.* Great.
The person whose head was incomplete burst into tears.
As it fell, what could the doll do? Nothing.
Go to sleep.
You look great in shorts. And the flag looks great too.
Everyone enjoyed the explosions.
Time to wake up.
But better get used to dreams.

Bob Perelman

Many readers find this text very confusing. They may look for a way of *reading* it – a way of making sense of the poem – that will give it a fixed, coherent meaning. In making readers conscious of this impulse, the poem exposes some of the expectations people have about poetry and the methods they use to read it.

Activities

1. In what ways (if any) does the poem disrupt *your* expectations? You might find the following questions useful for thinking about this.

    > Does the poem seem 'fragmented'?
    > Does it seem to lack a reason for being written?
    > Does it seem to lack structure?

    What do your answers demonstrate about your assumptions or expectations, in regard to poetry? Do your assumptions match any of the theories of poetry you have read about in this chapter?

2. Bob Perelman's poetry is part of a movement called 'Language Poetry'. It seems Perelman created his poem by making up captions for photographs in a book about China. Each caption is a sentence in the poem. This means that whatever coherence the poem has lies 'elsewhere' – in a book that the reader has no access to.

    Create your own Language Poem by drawing words and phrases from an existing text. Suitable texts could include:

    > – a list of top 40 songs, including the names of bands;
    > – a television program guide;
    > – headlines from a newspaper;
    > – lines from the index of a book.

    Construct a poem of about 20 lines, with a one-word title. You could share these poems through performance readings, or display them on a pin-board in your classroom.

Discussion

> There are no activities suggested here for *analysing* Perelman's poem.

> What activities would you normally expect to find in this section of the book?
> Can you suggest why there are none here for Perelman's poem?
> What might this say about the *relationship* between poetry, criticism, and education? (For example: what role do 'right answers' play in all of the above questions? What happens to each of them if the concept of 'right answers' is rejected?)

The last word?

Post-structuralism is by no means the last or newest word in theories of literature. Since the post-structural movement, ways of thinking about poetry have continued to change. One new branch of study focuses on the ways texts are actually *used* by people in specific situations, rather than on arguments about general links between poetry and language or poetry and society. This approach to poetry study has been suggested by the work of French philosopher Michel Foucault, and by other thinkers such as the Australian scholar Ian Hunter. These ideas about literature are an important influence on this book.

Wordsworth's sisters?

Much of the theory and criticism about poetry that has been preserved through history is written by men. This raises the question of whether our ideas about poetry have been shaped by the views and values of men to the exclusion of women's views.

While there are female theorists and critics, some women writers have rejected theoretical discussions of poetry because they see theory as a typically male way of thinking. The next writers make their point through their poems, which have a strong political or social message.

Wendy Cope: An Argument with Wordsworth

This poem by English poet Wendy Cope takes issue with one of William Wordsworth's statements about poetry. Read the poem, then do the activities that follow.

AN ARGUMENT WITH WORDSWORTH

'poetry ... takes its origin from emotion recollected in tranquillity'
Preface to *Lyrical Ballads*

People are always quoting that
and all of them seem to agree
And it's probably most unwise to admit
that it's different for me.
I have emotion –
no-one who knows me could fail to detect it
But there's a serious shortage of tranquillity
in which to recollect it.
So this is my contribution to the theoretical debate:
Sometimes poetry is emotion
recollected in a highly emotional state.

Wendy Cope

Activities

1. The following questions and answers may help you to discuss Wendy Cope's poem. Choose the answer or answers you agree with, then compare your choices with those of others in your class.

    a. Why might the speaker say it is 'unwise' to disagree with Wordsworth:

        – because Wordsworth is wiser than the speaker?
        – because so many people *think* Wordsworth is wiser?
        – because women's views carry less weight than men's?
        – some other reason?

    b. What might the speaker's reference to a 'shortage of tranquillity' imply:

        – that Wordsworth lived at a time when life was less hectic than now?
        – that Wordsworth had a privileged lifestyle and did not need to work?
        – that women's lives are more hectic than men's?
        – something else?

    c. What do you imagine the speaker's tone to be:

        – calm and reasonable?   – hysterical?
        – angry?   – indignant?
        – amused?   – other?

        What are the reasons for your choice?

2. Although the poem claims to argue with Wordsworth, there are points on which it seems to agree with him. What are these points?

Lynn Peters: Why Dorothy Wordsworth is not as Famous

The poet William Wordsworth had a sister, Dorothy, who he lived with for some time in the English Lake District. Dorothy Wordsworth (1771–1855) was a skilled writer and diarist, though none of her works was published in her own lifetime. Except for the journals she kept about her brother William's life and writings, Dorothy's own work has gone largely unrecognised.

The following poem builds on these facts to make a point about history's neglect of women writers. It is by English poet Lynn Peters.

Read the poem, then do the activities that follow.

WHY DOROTHY WORDSWORTH IS NOT AS FAMOUS AS HER BROTHER

'I wandered lonely as a ...
They're in the top drawer, William,
Under your socks –
I wandered lonely as a –
No not that drawer, the top one.
I wandered by myself –
Well wear the ones you can find,
No don't get overwrought my dear,
I'm coming.'

'I was out one day wandering
Lonely as a cloud when –
Softboiled egg, yes my dear
As usual, three minutes –
As a cloud when all of a sudden –
Look, I said I'll cook it,
Just hold on will you –
All right, I'm coming.'

'One day I was out for a walk
When I saw this flock –
It can't be too hard, it had three minutes.
Well put some butter on it.
– This host of golden daffodils
As I was out for a stroll one –'

'Oh you fancy a stroll, do you.
Yes, all right William. I'm coming.
It's on the peg. Under your hat.
I'll bring my pad, shall I, in case
You want to jot something down?'

Lynn Peters

1. Lynn Peters' poem is an effective piece to read aloud. Work with a partner to prepare a presentation of the poem. You could experiment with the following approaches.

   a. Changing your tone of voice to indicate the shifts between poetry and conversation.
   b. Trying different ways of presenting the speaker (patient, hassled, bitter, and so on).
   c. Making the poetry sound more and more muddled as the interruptions increase.

2. This poem is often read as a 'feminist' text. Which of the following readings do you think best fit the poem? (Make a note of your choices.)

   a. Dorothy Wordsworth's work was stolen by her brother.
   b. Dorothy Wordsworth voluntarily sacrificed her personal ambitions for her brother.
   c. Society expected Dorothy Wordsworth to sacrifice her personal ambitions for her brother.
   d. Society expects all women to sacrifice their interests for others.
   e. As a poet, Dorothy Wordsworth was the equal of her famous brother.
   f. Women are the equals of men in many fields, but their efforts are stifled.

   Explain your reasons for reading the poem in this way.

Your theory

In this chapter you have seen that ideas about poetry change from time to time and place to place. So, too, do the types of poetry that people write and read. These ideas and practices are shaped by complex forces, such as historical events, changing lifestyles and values, and so on.

Your own ideas about poetry will have been shaped by these forces, too. Some of the factors that have shaped your views might include:

   – your social background (culture, parents' attitudes, etc);
   – your gender (whether you are male or female);
   – your educational background (what you have been taught in the past);
   – your peer group (your friends and their attitudes).

This means that your attitudes to poetry may reflect attitudes and beliefs held by many people in your community. One way of exploring these attitudes and beliefs is to try setting out your own theory of poetry.

Activities

1. Try thinking through your own theory by writing your response to the following questions.

   a. What is the nature of poetry?

      (Is it an imitation of the world? An expression of personal feeling? An 'open text'? A category of writing? Something else?)

   b. What makes a 'good' poem?

      (Truth or accuracy? Verbal cleverness? Language that readers understand? A moral lesson? Different factors?)

   c. What is a poet?

      (Anyone who chooses to write poetry? A person with special insight? Someone who is 'inspired' by a Muse? A 'mixer of writings'?)

d. What do/should readers gain from poetry?

    (A moral lesson? Enjoyment? Understanding? Discrimination? Nothing?)

e. What is the value of poetry?

    (Is it a civilising influence? A dangerous activity? An irrelevance?)

Share your answers in discussion, and compare your views with those of others in your class. Is there a general agreement, or are there differences of view? What might account for these differences and similarities?

2. Find a poem that you like, and consider how it relates to your theory about the nature and value of poetry.

3. To test your grasp of the theories you have studied, browse through some poetry anthologies and find examples of poems that each of the theorists above would approve (or disapprove) of. These could be collected for a class display.

Writing

1. Write your own 'reply' to one of the theorists in this chapter, setting out your view of what poetry is and what value (if any) it has. In planning your response, you can make use of the notes you have made in working through this chapter.

2. Try writing a poetic argument in response to one of the theorists below. You can use Wendy Cope's poem as a model for your own. Use one of the following statements as a starting point, or choose your own quotation. (You may paraphrase or shorten the statement.)

'all poetical imitations are ruinous' – *Plato*

'Imitation is one instinct in our nature.' – *Aristotle*

'it is always a writer's duty to make the world better' – *Samuel Johnson*

'A poem must not mean but be' – *W.K. Wimsatt & M.C. Beardsley*

'The text is a tissue of quotations' – *Roland Barthes*

Use the title 'An Argument With – ' and follow Wendy Cope's structure.

Talking

Present a talk on a poem you have read, showing how it relates to your views of the nature and value of poetry. Your talk should include:

- a brief introduction about the poem and your theory (eg, title, poet, some details about your view of poetry);

- a prepared reading of the poem;

- a copy of the text for your audience (on overhead film, hand-outs, or a large poster);

- an explanation of how the poem illustrates or supports your views (or how it fails to do so).

Another look at your summary chart

Go back to the chart at the beginning of this chapter on page 131. You should now be able to fill in the details more successfully by drawing on the things you have learned by studying different theories of poetry.

Answers

Chapter 1

The layout of the texts on page 13 is as follows:

> A man who weighed many an ounce
> Used language I dare not pronounce,
> For a fellow unkind,
> Pulled his chair from behind,
> Just to see, so he said, if he'd bounce.
>
> *(Limerick, Anonymous)*

> On the planet of Nim in the quadrant of Zax
> lives a blue-bearded Bodge that the locals call Max.
> He lives all alone in a ramshackle duff
> and he spends his days lunching on yaffetter fluff.
> Now a Bodge is a very strange creature indeed
> for his body is covered in Evergreen weed
> (it's a little like mould and a little like moss
> and a little like lichen – except for the gloss)
> But a bearded Bodge, well he's one of a kind
> and his Evergreen coat, although shortish behind,
> sweeps down from his chin like a river of gold,
> (except that it's *blue* as I'm sure you've been told).
>
> *('The Bearded Bodge,' Dr Brain)*

> The sea is calm tonight.
> The tide is full, the moon lies fair
> Upon the straits; – on the French coast the light
> Gleams and is gone; the cliffs of England stand,
> Glimmering and vast, out in the tranquil bay.
> Come to the window, sweet is the night-air!
> Only, from the long line of spray
> Where the sea meets the moon-blanch'd land,
> Listen! you hear the grating roar
> Of pebbles which the waves draw back, and fling,
> At their return, up the high strand,
> Begin, and cease, and then again begin,
> With tremulous cadence slow, and bring
> The eternal note of sadness in.
>
> *(From 'Dover Beach,' Matthew Arnold)*

Chapter 3

1. 'Mushrooms' by Sylvia Plath on page 54 (the words have been run together to hinder accidental reading): acquirebetrayssoftvoicelessshadowaskingmeeknudgersinherit. See also page 152 for the poem as written by Sylvia Plath.
2. 'The Earth Lover' by Katharine Susannah Prichard on page 56: Versethreeistheoriginalverse. See also page 153 for the poem as written by Katharine Susannah Prichard.

Chapter 4

1. The poems on page 76 are: 1. 'Sonnet 61', Michael Drayton (sonnet); 2. 'The Warning', A. Crapsey (cinquain); 3. 'Waiting', Shiki (haiku); 4. 'The Knight' from *The Canterbury Tales*, Geoffrey Chaucer (heroic couplets); 5. From 'The Rape of the Lock', Alexander Pope (heroic couplets); 6. Untitled, Kikaku (haiku); 7. 'Triad', A. Crapsey (cinquain); 8. 'Sonnet 10', John Donne (sonnet).
2. Missing lines from Shakespeare's 'Sonnet 130' on page 83: 1. Than in the breath that from my mistress reeks. 2. That music hath a far more pleasing sound.

MUSHROOMS

Overnight, very
Whitely, discreetly,
Very quietly

Our toes, our noses
Take hold on the loam,
Acquire the air.

Nobody sees us,
Stops us, betrays us,
The small grains make room.

Soft fists insist on
Heaving the needles,
The leafy bedding,

Even the paving.
Our hammers, our rams,
Earless and eyeless,

Perfectly voiceless,
Widen the crannies,
Shoulder through holes. We

Diet on water,
On crumbs of shadow,
Bland mannered, asking

Little or nothing.
So many of us!
So many of us!

We are shelves, we are
Tables, we are meek,
We are edible,

Nudgers and shovers
In spite of ourselves.
Our kind multiplies:

We shall by morning
Inherit the earth.
Our foot's in the door.

Sylvia Plath

THE EARTH LOVER

Let me lie in the grass –
Bathe in its verdure
As one bathes in the sea –
Soul-drowned in herbage,
The essence of clover,
Dandelion, camomile, knapweed
And centaury.

Let me lie close to the earth,
Battened against the broad breast
Which brings all things to being
And gives rest to all things.

Let me inspire the odours of birth,
Death, living,
Sweets of the mould,
The generative sap of insects,
Crushed in grasses, witch weeds,
Flowering herbs.

For I am an earth child,
An earth lover,
And I ask no more than to be,
Of the earth, earthy,
And to mingle again with the divine dust.

Katharine Susannah Prichard

Acknowledgments and sources

Cover:
With kind permission of the artist, 'Buch mit zwei Augen' by Hubertus Gojowczyk © 1969, the artist.

Poems:
The publishers acknowledge the sources of the poems appearing in *Studying Poetry* and thank the following where appropriate for permission to use copyright material.

Deborah Andrews, for 'The Curse of the Pear-Shaped Figure', 'Middle-Aged Spread' and 'The Good Lord', from *For Alan Jackson*; Basher for 'Tree Frogs': © 1997, the author; 'The Tyger' by William Blake, from *Considering Poetry*, B.A. Phythian, English Universities Press, 1970, pp.93–97. (British Museum); Little Brown & Company for 'I Poet' by Jean Binta Breeze, from *Spring Cleaning*, Virago Press Ltd.; Thanks to Bogle L'Ouverture Press and Valerie Bloom for 'Yuh Hear Bout?' by Valerie Bloom © 1993 from *Touch Mi, Tell Mi*; 'The Soldier' by Rupert Brooke from *The Poetical Works of Rupert Brooke* Edited by Geoffrey Keynes. Faber and Faber, Ltd; 1946 h/bk 1970 p/bk; Pete Brown and Fulcrum Press for 'Reckless', © 1969 Fulcrum Press; from *Let 'em Roll Kafka*, by Pete Brown, Fulcrum Press; 'Seasons' by Jessica Cameron, from *A Phantom Script*. Edited by Brian Keyte & Richard Baines. Melbourne: Nelson, 1986; 'The Knight' by Geoffrey Chaucer, from *Canterbury Tales*. Translated by Nevill Coghill. London: Guild Publishing, 1986; 'An Argument with Wordsworth' by Wendy Cope, from *Serious Concerns*, Faber and Faber Ltd. Grateful acknowledgment to the author and to Faber and Faber Ltd; 'Triad' and 'The Warning' by Algernon Crapsey, from *Verse*. New York: Alfred Knopf Inc. © Adelaide Crapsey; 'r-p-o-p-h-e-s-s-a-g-r' is reprinted from COMPLETE POEMS 1904–1962, by E.E. Cummings, edited by George J. Firmage, by permission of W.W. Norton & Company. Copyright © 1991 by the Trustees for the E.E. Cummings Trust and George James Firmage; 'Elegy for Drowned Children' by Bruce Dawe from *Sometimes Gladness: Collected Poems 1954-82.* (Revised edition, 1978) Longman. By kind permission of the publisher, Addison Wesley Longman Australia, and the author, Bruce Dawe; 'Gutter Press' by Paul Dehn © James Bernard. From *Visible Voices*. Edited by Michael Jones, and published by Channel 4 Learning. By kind permission of James Bernard; 'Out, Out-' from THE POETRY OF ROBERT FROST. Edited by Edward Connery Latham. Jonathon Cape. With grateful acknowledgment to The Estate of Robert Frost, the editor Edward Connery Latham and the publisher Jonathon Cape; 'I'd Like' by Piet Hein, © Piet Hein, from *Grooks* by Piet Hein. Reproduced by permission of the publisher Hodder & Stoughton Ltd; Haiku by Basho, Chora, Chosu, Kikaku and others, and for 'Waiting' by Shiki, from AN INTRODUCTION TO HAIKU by Harold G. Henderson. Copyright © 1958. Used by permission of Doubleday, a division of Bantam Doubleday Dell Publishing Group, Inc.; Gerard Manly Hopkins, 'Spring and Fall': © 1967 The Society of Jesus and Oxford University Press, from *The Poems of Gerard Manly Hopkins*, 4th ed, ed. W.H. Gardner and N.H. Mackenzie; Tom Jones and Harvey Schmidt, from 'Try to Remember': © 1960 Tom Jones and Harvey Schmidt, Warner Chappell Music Ltd; 'Toads' by Philip Larkin is reprinted from *The Less Deceived* by kind permission of The Marvell Press, England and Australia; 'The Rainwalkers' by Denise Levertov from *With Eyes at the Back of Our Heads* from SELECTED POEMS. Grateful acknowledgment to Denise Levertov-Goodman, Bloodaxe Books and New directions Publishing Corporation, New York; 'The Horses' by Edwin Muir, from COLLECTED POEMS, 1921–1958. With grateful acknowledgment to Faber and Faber; Dennis O'Driscoll, 'Misunderstanding and Muzak': © 1993 from *Long Story Short*, Anvil Press Poetry Ltd; Wilfred Owen, 'Anthem for Doomed Youth': Taken from *Considering Poetry*, B.A. Phythian, English Universities Press, 1970, pp.99–101. The British Museum, Harold Owen, and Chatto & Windus; Monty Python extracts from *The Brand New Monty Python Book* © 1973 by Michael Palin, Graham Chapman, John Cleese, Eric Idle, Terry Jones and Terry Gilliam. Published by Methuen. Acknowledgments to Random House UK Ltd; Bob Perelman, 'China' from *Primer*, This Press, Berkeley, no date; 'Why Dorothy Wordsworth is Not as Famous as Her Brother' by Lynn Peters. © Lynn Peters, 1993. First published in *Cosmopolitan* magazine. Reprinted by kind permission of the author, Lynn Peters, and The Lisa Everleigh Agency. Grateful acknowledgment for 'Mushrooms' by Sylvia Plath, from 'The Colossus' from COLLECTED POEMS, edited by Ted Hughes, published by Faber & Faber Ltd and for 'Mirror' by Sylvia Plath from 'Crossing the Water', COLLECTED POEMS, edited by Ted Hughes, published by Faber & Faber Ltd.; 'From the Lighthouse' by Flora Podmore, © Flora Podmore published by Chalkface Press. By kind permission of the author; Kim Poulton, 'Charges and Payment'. © 1996 Kim Poulton; 'How to Paint the Portrait of a Bird' by Jacques Prevert. Translation by Paul Dehn. © James Bernard. From *Romantic Landscape*, Hamish Hamilton. By kind permission of James Bernard; 'To Paint the Portrait of a Bird' by Jacques Prevert. English translation © 1958 by Lawrence Ferlinghetti. From *Paroles*. Reprinted by permission of CITY LIGHTS BOOKS; 'The Earth Lover' by Katharine Susannah Prichard, from *The Earth Lover and Other Verses* © 1932, Sunnybrook Publications. Reprinted 1990. Kind permission of Mr Ric Throssell, and Curtis Brown (Australia) Pty Ltd, Sydney; 'Thinking about Heaven', John Richmond by kind permission of the author; 'The Affair' by Alan Riddell, © Alan Riddell, from *Eclipse*. Published by Calder and Boyars. By kind permission of the author and Calder Publications Ltd, 126 Cornwall Road, London SE1 8TQ, ENGLAND; Annette Ross, 'My Country', © 1997. By kind permission of the author; Grateful acknowledgment for 'Untitled poem' by Shoha from *The Four Seasons*. Translated by Peter Beilenson. Published by Peter Pauper Press, New York, 1958; 'Thanks' by Gael Turnbull is from *A Trampoline*, published by Jonathan Cape & Cape Goliard. Reprinted with the kind permission of the author and Jonathon Cape Publishers; 'First Ice' by Andrei Voznesensky. Translated by George Reavey: from NEW RUSSIAN POETS. Kind permission of Marion Boyars Publishers Ltd.; Andrei Voznesensky, 'First Frost'. Trans. by Stanley Kunitz. 'This Letter's to Say' by Raymond Wilson, from *Visible Voices*. Edited by Michael Jones, Channel 4 Learning. Reproduced by kind permission of Mrs G.M. Wilson © 1994; William Wordsworth, 'I Wandered Lonely as a Cloud' from *Selected Poems and Prefaces*. Edited by Jack Stillinger, 1966, Boston: Houghton Mifflin Company.

Critical works:
The critical works in Chapter Six have been extracted and adapted from the following:

Plato. 'The Republic, Book X.' Translated by B. Jowett. *The Portable Plato*. Ed. Scott Buchanan. Penguin: Harmondsworth, England 1976. pp.658–674; Aristotle. 'Poetics'. Translated by S.H. Butcher. *The Great Critics: An Anthology of Literary Criticism*. Ed. James Harry Smith and Edd Winfield Parks. 3rd ed. New York: Norton, 1967. pp.28–61; Samuel Johnson, 'Preface to Shakespeare.' *The Great Critics: An Anthology of Literary Criticism*. Ed. James Harry Smith and Edd Winfield Parks. 3rd ed. New York: Norton, 1967. pp.443–460; W.K. Wimsatt, and Monroe C. Beardsley, 'The Intentional Fallacy.' *20th Century Literary Criticism: A Reader*. Ed David Lodge. Longman: 1972. Roland Barthes, 'The Death of the Author.' Trans. Stephen Heath. *Image-Music-Text*. London: Fontana: 1979. pp.142–8.

Index of first lines

Index of first lines: continued

Index of Poems – by title

Index of Poems – by author

Notes: